D0457308

talk to strangers

How Everyday Random Encounters Can Expand Your Business, Career, Income, and Life

David Topus

WILEY

John Wiley & Sons, Inc.

ISBN 978-1-118-20347-7 (cloth); ISBN 978-1-118-22841-8 (ebk);
ISBN 978-1-118-23762-5 (ebk); ISBN 978-1-118-26547-5 (ebk)

Printed in the United States of America
10 9 8 7 6 5 4 3 2 1

Contents

Contents

Acknowledgments

How can one ever thank everyone who has helped him or her be successful with work when there are *so* many who contribute, both directly and indirectly? I remember awhile back encountering an artist in a park who was painting a beautiful landscape scene of the trees and benches. I stopped, admired the painting, commented on how pretty it was, and then asked him how long it took him to paint that scene. "Twenty two years," he said, explaining that it took that long to develop and refine the skill, and therefore, to create beautiful works of art. Of course, I stayed in touch and he became a friend; and yes, I bought art from him over the years.

But his original point always stuck with me—whatever we're doing now is a cumulative result of everyone who has ever influenced us. I personally would have to thank everyone I ever met in a random encounter for giving me the benefit of the doubt, and even those who didn't, for they forced me to sharpen my random connecting skills. Beyond that, my thanks go first to friend and colleague Walt Kuenstler, who insisted I make that phone call and then tell my story and whose unwavering enthusiasm and encouragement were instrumental in motivating me to write—and continue writing—this book. I have to acknowledge my parents, from whom I learned social versatility, a skill that undoubtedly accounts for my inclination to talk to just about everyone I come across.

To the fine folks at Wiley I offer my great appreciation—first and foremost, Lauren Murphy, who "got it" right off the bat and moved the proposal quickly and successfully through the process, not to mention, was always gladly there for me with answers and assistance; Christine Moore, for her ever-positive, cheery disposition, as well as great copy points; Deborah Schindlar, who so competently turned my words into a book; and Peter Knox, for his marketing insights. Thanks to Gretchen Kelly, proposal writer extraordinaire, and my agent, Katharine Sands, who helped me learn the ropes without having to fall too far. To my wide circle of friends, colleagues, and associates, I offer my thanks for their ongoing interest and support. And finally, to my life mate Deborah, who encouraged, supported, and guided me from the very inception of the book and whose patience and creativity made the entire process so much easier and the outcome so much better than it would have been otherwise—and who, you guessed it, I met in a luggage store at the mall.

Guide to Charts, Tables, and Lists

Introduction

There's always something to say.

No matter where you are, who you're with, or what's happening around you, you can make an observation, ask a question, or share a thought with a stranger. And when you do, you tap into a world of unlimited possibilities you never knew existed until that moment.

I should admit that I've been striking up conversations with strangers through chance encounters and staying in touch with them for a long time. So although it might seem a bit extreme that I've remained in contact with the doctor who delivered me into this world many decades ago, it's simply how I began my habit of meeting, talking to, and connecting with strangers for the better part of my life. Over the latter years, I have earned hundreds of thousands of dollars in consulting and training fees and have built long-term, mutually profitable relationships with people I met in the most random of ways: on planes, in coffee shops, in restaurants, in hotel lobbies, at weddings, in elevators, in doctors' offices, and just about everywhere else I've been.

Talking to strangers comes naturally to me. And although the results have been remarkable, I can't tell you for sure exactly what has driven this behavior since a young age, except that I always found people available to me—willing to smile back, to acknowledge a common experience in the moment, to share pieces of the stories of their lives, and to teach, guide, and help me. I also have an insatiable curiosity about the people I encounter wherever I go. I want to know: Where are they from? Where are they going? What do they do? Who *are* they? I'm always fascinated by their answers, even the ones who don't appear all that interesting on the surface.

I've always had a desire to connect with the people around me. I didn't have much of an outcome in mind when I was younger, except perhaps to help someone, learn something, or make a friend. I would always find a reason to circle back with a particular person long after our initial meeting, sometimes to find out what that person was up to, sometimes just to let that person know what I was doing, and sometimes simply to say hello. Some of these new connections faded away over time, and some I still know to this day—30 and 40 years later.

One early random encounter comes to mind that in many ways laid the groundwork for a lifetime of talking to strangers that would become relationships of great positive impact. It was a perfect example of the idea that you never know who you'll meet unless you make yourself available. As a teenager, my sister and I had summer jobs in Manhattan, and we would take the bus to the subway into the city. Often the traffic would be so heavy that cars would sit bumper to bumper in front of the bus stop. One morning while waiting for the bus I made eye contact with an executive-looking man who was driving an expensive car and was undoubtedly headed in the same direction we were.

After a smile and gesture of friendliness, he opened his passenger window and asked if we were going into the city. I said yes, he offered a lift, and feeling safe in accepting, we hopped in. What began as a serendipitous ride turned into a long-term friendship with the managing partner of the fourth largest stock brokerage firm in the country. Someone who for years and years I would visit in his office (nab a free sandwich in his company cafeteria—after all, I *was* a high school student with a summer job!), but most importantly, from whom I would learn about business and have a model for business success. And maybe that was at a safer time, when taking a ride from a stranger didn't require a credit check and the last four digits of the driver's Social Security number. But the story is true and the message is clear: what starts as a random encounter and opportunity can become a long-term friendship and growth experience, all because of a smile, a gesture of friendliness, and a willingness to take a chance.

Whereas meeting people in random encounters was more of a natural inclination, even a hobby, during my younger years, it became a critical skill as I entered the business world. I discovered that the more I reached out to strangers, the more I found people who had a need for my services. As a result, my ability to connect with people by way of casual, everyday encounters became invaluable in building my career and financial success. You might call me a consummate networker in today's language. However, I do this for a much more important reason than that. I do this because it transforms my everyday world into one big untapped opportunity to expand and enrich virtually every aspect of my life, while simultaneously providing value to those I meet in return.

I realized over the years that just by sparking a conversation with someone, I would learn all kinds of things about that person—and concurrently discover ways that I could be of service. I found that the more I made myself available to people, the more opportunities came my way.

These random encounters were so productive as I was developing my business that I began engaging in what some might consider a peculiar undertaking: I started flying around the country, to no particular destination, but rather to meet potential clients along the way. I would travel to places far and wide: Atlanta to Boston. New York to Chicago. Dallas to LA and Seattle. Detroit to Tokyo. Often I would take the most circuitous route. And it really didn't matter where I was going, only that there would be businesspeople along the route. There was nothing waiting for me in any of these places; all the action was in the airport, on the plane, on the tram, in the taxi, and in the hotel lobby.

And so for me, flying around the globe to make business contacts was no big deal; it was just my marketing strategy. But my friends and colleagues saw it as something unusual and insisted that I should tell my story. My first call was to Joe Sharkey, who writes the business travel column of the *New York Times*. I immediately received a return call. "You do *what?*" he asked.

"Well," I replied, "I take flights all over the country and sometimes around the world, just to meet potential clients." Joe said something about that being the most incredible thing he'd ever heard. An interview followed that afternoon, and my story appeared in the next edition of his column.

As is my natural inclination, I spent much of my time writing this book in public places, surrounded by complete strangers. I worked in coffee shops, on airplanes, in hotel lobbies, in parks, in libraries, and in restaurants. As I look around, I see unlimited opportunity in the people in sight. Walking, talking potential . . . in every one of them.

I am also actively communicating with at least four prospective clients as I write, all of whom I met through completely random encounters. One was at a coffee shop, two were seatmates on flights, and one I met in an office building elevator. I anticipate that at least two of them will monetize significantly.

You can do the same. This book will show you how you can expand your pool of contacts to enhance your business, career, and personal life. It's closely connected to the broader issue of personal branding or self-marketing, where you take control of your success by managing who you know and who knows you—except in this case, you will be going beyond your typical and somewhat predictable networking venues. You will discover how you can easily and naturally connect with the people with whom you come in contact throughout your daily life.

Of course, you may not choose to go to the lengths that I do to meet people. But whether you go halfway around the world to make random connections or find them within a 20-mile radius of your home, at the end of the day (actually at the beginning of the day and all day long), it is about seeing the world as one big opportunity, where everyone you meet can enrich your life in some way or another—and you, theirs. It is about taking advantage of every opportunity to make face-to-face, in-person connections and leveraging them for mutual benefit, wherever you find yourself.

The woman in front of you in line at the supermarket, the guy sitting next to you on an airplane, your fellow conference attendees, the person sitting in the lobby, other guests at the wedding, the others on the shuttle van—these are the "people portals" of your life. They're the individuals who just may be able to lead you to personal and professional success—that is, *if* you know how to connect and cultivate them.

And as you'll discover while reading this book, everybody you encounter either *is* somebody you want to know or *knows* somebody you want to know. Some random encounters lead somewhere specific; others take a circuitous route. Whether you're a salesperson, job candidate, small-business owner, independent consultant, recent college grad, or new to your community, you'll doubtlessly find that the more widely you reach out to people, the more likely you will be to discover new possibilities. In fact, expanding your network of contacts is one of the few activities you can control to put the odds of success in your favor. And the best part? These leads don't cost you anything, and they're open to you every day. You just have to know how to recognize, cultivate, and optimize them.

In many ways, this book is a field guide, a resource you can take with you and refer to when you are out and about, surrounded by random connecting possibilities. So read on to find out how you can tap into a world of opportunity that is available to you day and night. These opportunities are free for the asking and can lead you to new clients, new career opportunities, new insights, and new friends—as well as to the financial and personal rewards that follow from making such fortuitous connections.

SECTION

I

Creating Your Future Through the People You Haven't Even Met...Yet

You never know who is at the table across the room from you, standing in line behind you, or sitting in the seat next to you. It could be your biggest new client, your next employer, the gateway to a piece of information that changes your life, or the best friend you ever make.

Sometimes the most valuable encounters occur in the most unlikely, unexpected places. You can't plan them, you can't predict them. But you *can* create them. You just don't know what's possible; that is, you don't know until you ask.

1

The Untapped Potential in Your Everyday Encounters

If you're reading this in a public place with people nearby, take a look around and observe them. If you're not in public, make a point of doing this the next time you are. Find someone who looks interesting, and think of something you could say to engage that person in conversation. It could be a comment or question about what the other is doing or what's happening where you both are at that moment. It could be something that intrigues you about the other person about which you'd like to know more. Maybe you overheard part of a phone call that leads you to think he or she is in the same business as you. Maybe the person is carrying a backpack with a conference name and date embossed that is intriguing to you or wearing a unique or especially attractive piece of jewelry. Chances are if you approach the person respectfully, you can successfully initiate a conversation. Then, in that very instant, you will have opened the door to possibilities you didn't even know existed until you took a chance by talking to a stranger.

I did this very thing a few years ago during a quiet Sunday afternoon flight from Boston Logan Airport, hardly the time or place you would expect to make two of the most lucrative business connections of a lifetime. But it was, and the results were measured in six figures and ongoing access to a huge network of business opportunities.

Nothing seemed unusual as I was standing near the gate waiting to board the plane, except that the gate agents seemed to be working extra hard to create a smooth boarding experience. *Hmm*, I thought, *someone important must be on this flight.* I didn't see any celebrities or luminaries, at least not that I could recognize. The boarding process continued for our full flight, and when I finally sat in my seat I turned to the person next to me and said, "*If* I ever get the chance to meet this airline's CEO, I will have to tell him what a great job his Boston people are doing." My seatmate leaned toward me, pointed across the aisle, and whispered in my ear, "Well, you will have your chance…he's sitting right there."

It is a rare moment indeed to find yourself sitting an airplane aisle away from the CEO of that very airline—the third-largest airline in the world; it's even *more* unusual to have the CEO of a leading hotel chain sitting next to you and pointing out that the airline CEO is, in fact, sitting three feet away. But it happened, just like that—all because I talked to a stranger.

When you're a sales consultant with a background in transportation and a random encounter like this presents itself, there's only one thing to do: make the connections, one across the aisle and one sitting next to me. I monetized both within a matter of months.

I had wanted to do business with in this airline for a long time, but I found that it was very difficult to gain access to someone at this level by utilizing the normal channels. Sure, I could call his office and try to get an appointment, but as an unknown consultant, I would have little likelihood of getting one. I could send an e-mail, but chances are it would be intercepted, if it even got past the company's spam filter. I could wait in the company parking lot and approach him as he walked into the building, but in that case I would be more likely to end up meeting the company's security staff than the CEO. Yet here he was, sitting mere feet away from me; it was my chance—on a quiet Sunday afternoon and the relaxed attitude that goes along with it.

Since he was across the aisle a few rows up, I couldn't initiate conversation easily, and I didn't want to interrupt him while he was working. I would need the flight attendant to deliver my request for a chat so that he could agree and then determine the right time and place. Moments later she returned with the good news: yes, sure, he would be happy to talk with me—in the Jetway, once we were on the ground.

Once we had landed, we stood together just outside the aircraft, with his shuttle van and entourage of assistants waiting. Here I was, face to face with the CEO of a major global transportation company, getting the once-in-a-lifetime opportunity to leverage a completely random connection. After a few pleasantries about the trip we had both just taken, I complimented the great job his Boston crew did, explained that I had done consulting work for one of their competitors a few years prior. I went on to tell him that I had a unique approach to getting corporate travel contracts and that I would appreciate some guidance on how to get my program into the company.

He responded by tearing off the seat assignment portion of his ticket and writing down his phone number along with the name of the person in charge of sales development. "Tell her I suggested you get in touch," he said. "And that I thought the idea is worth a close look."

That single, random encounter led to a multiyear, six-figure consulting and training engagement that grew into a long-term relationship with the company, a number of its business units, and a variety of great client friends, many of whom have gone on to other companies and brought me in to work for them there, too. It also led to a smaller but equally rewarding project for the hotel CEO who was sitting next to me and pointed me toward the airline exec.

The opportunities that await you in the people you encounter throughout your day are far-reaching and unpredictable—making them all the more exciting and intriguing. The people you don't even know yet can expand your world in many ways. Which of the following do you want to do?

- Uncover a prospect.
- Sell a new client.
- Land a new and/or better job.
- Get the name of a contact in a prospective company.
- Gain access to an influential person in your industry.
- Be informed about a company moving to the area.
- Hear about a franchise opportunity.
- Learn about new products or services in your marketplace.
- Find out about an industry networking group.
- Discover information about a new career.
- Pick up a tip about how to use the Internet to brand yourself.
- Learn about a new application of technology.
- Find out about a competitor.
- Enlist a new supplier.
- Come up with a new marketing approach.
- Meet an investor.
- Recruit an employee.
- Strike up a strategic business alliance.
- Hear about a book or article that could change your life.
- Discover something about your community.
- Find out about a new restaurant or bar (where you could make *more* random connections).
- Meet a new accountant, dentist, doctor, attorney, Realtor, home repair person, or other personal service provider.
- Become aware of a better school for your children.
- Make a friend.

All you have to do is look in front of you, behind you, beside you, and across from you. And then with a simple acknowledgment—a nod, a smile, a question, or comment, you can unearth unlimited potential.

Chapter at a Glance

- You never know who's around you, until you ask.
- You could be sitting or standing next to the CEO of a major corporation or next to someone who can introduce you to someone of great influence.
- The people you meet in random encounters represent endless possibilities.

2

New Faces in New Places

There are potential new contacts and relationships to be made wherever you find people. If you were to take an inventory of every place you go over the period of a week, you'd realize that your life is full of these kinds of "new places, new faces" situations. Think about it for a moment: how many different venues do you visit over the course of your daily (and weekly) life? Supermarkets, car washes, dry cleaners, restaurants, pharmacies, shopping malls, golf courses, office supply stores, barber shops, hair and nail salons, kids' sporting events, banks, bookstores, and bars (although maybe not in that order). These are all fertile ground for random connecting. And that's only a partial list of places—with every one having potentially lucrative contacts to be made. This list doesn't even cover special occasions, such as weddings, parties, conferences, luncheons, business trips, and so on—events where opportunities for making connections and meeting new people are as plentiful as the air you breathe.

Keep in mind that although you *can* meet someone new everywhere you go, some places are more conducive than others for striking up relationships. Venues where social interaction is expected and desired, such as coffee shops, bars, parties, weddings, and industry events, are most conducive. There is less of a sense of assumed access and availability in places like a hotel front desk, shuttle buses, airplanes, elevators, doctor's offices, bookstores, and sporting events. But regardless of the implied social availability, you can make a connection anywhere—that is, if you believe you can.

Of course, some venues are more likely to attract and therefore provide more qualified connections than others. But over the course of a week, you will be presented with chances to meet hundreds of people, many of whom can become—or can lead you to—profitable business, and even personal, relationships.

I have met hundreds of people over the years in some of the most random, unusual, and often fleeting situations. Each venue offers different opportunities and challenges for random connecting. Throughout the book you will read about random encounters taking place in many of these venues, but for now here's a list that shows just how many different ones are available to you, and what to keep in mind about each one so that you maximize their potential for meeting people who can change your life.

Table 2.1 summarizes the various scenarios and settings in which I've met people over the years. This gives you a brief snapshot of the kind of encounter you might expect to have, along with the pros and cons and other details of each.

Chapter at a Glance

- In the course of your daily life, you visit dozens of venues.
- Some venues are more conducive than others to meeting people.
- You can meet people at any of them if you believe you can.

Table 2.1 The Pluses and Minuses of Various Random Connecting Venues

Venue	Pros	Cons	Likelihood of Finding Qualified Leads	Availability Factor (how available people are to connect)	Skill Level Required	Best Meeting Place(s)
Weddings	Large number of people; highly social; everyone friendly; plenty of booze	People aren't thinking about business; plenty of booze	Medium	High	Low	Bar; pre-ceremony; sitting at table for dinner; shuttles between events or to and from hotel
Airports and airplanes	Extensive time; uninterrupted; full attention	You could end up next to a dud; some people prefer to sleep	High	Medium	Medium	Galley; next seat

(continued)

11

Table 2.1 Continued

Venue	Pros	Cons	Likelihood of Finding Qualified Leads	Availability Factor (how available people are to connect)	Skill Level Required	Best Meeting Place(s)
Coffee shops	Wide cross section of people; many professional-minded	Many unemployed or trying to sell something	Medium	High	Low	In line; seating area
Industry conferences/ conventions	Huge number of people; buyers and sellers	Sometimes hard to distinguish between buyers and sellers; so much competition for attention customers don't remember you; everybody friendly, hard to calibrate *real* opportunities	High	High	Low	Hotel lobby; show floor; receptions; in transit

Doctor's offices	Extensive time	Everybody's sick, so they aren't feeling very sociable	Low	Low	High	Reception area; *not* exam room
Office building elevators	Contained environment; business-oriented	Limited time, depending on floor on which people enter/depart; works best if you and one other person are present	Medium to high	Low	Very high	Anywhere between lobby and top floor
Copy shops	Wide cross section of people; business-oriented	Limited time	Medium	Medium	High	Self-copy machines; customer service counter; book rack
Parties and social gatherings	People are happy; social environment	Not business-oriented	Medium to low, depending on host	High	Low	All; kitchen if at home

(continued)

Table 2.1 Continued

Venue	Pros	Cons	Likelihood of Finding Qualified Leads	Availability Factor (how available people are to connect)	Skill Level Required	Best Meeting Place(s)
Reunions	Common early life frame of reference; automatic affiliation	Many pretend to be more than they really are	Medium	High	Low	All

Get Out of Your Comfort Zone

Making successful random connections is about taking the path least traveled and planting new seeds in new fields. That is, the more you present yourself to the world—and the more you consciously choose to expand into unchartered territory—the more people you will meet.

It's a lot like the process of organic farming, which is based on getting the greatest concentration of nutrients from the soil, rather than planting over and over in the same earth. Although you can grow the vegetable in same ground time after time, you won't get the optimal nutritional value. Successful random networking, like successful farming, comes to fruition when you seek new connections in high-quality fresh fields.

Unfortunately, we humans are creatures of habit, so we tend to plant in the same garden. We take the same routes, stop at the same places (at the same time of day!), sit in the same place at the bar, sit in the same pew at church (hopefully not in that order!), shop in the same stores, spend time with the same people, and attend the same events—and generally do what is easy and comfortable. Obviously, this won't expand your world nearly as quickly as if you venture beyond the usual. Successful networkers constantly step out of their venue comfort zones, even—maybe *especially*—when it doesn't come naturally.

Random networking takes effort. It requires that you discover and exploit that inner drive to push into the unpredictable, and often unknown, territory. But that's where the fun is—in the excitement of meeting someone new, discovering new possibilities, in a place that's off the beaten path.

If you sit in the same section of the train every day, stop at the same coffee shop, and go to your exhibit booth down the same convention hall aisle each day of the conference, you will probably see the same people. It's easy. It's comfortable. It's safe. It's predictable. But it isn't going to expand your world.

Although random encounters are unplanned by definition, there *are* steps you can take to increase the likelihood of making these interactions successful. It requires some effort, energy, and even strategy, but mostly, it means that you put yourself in the right place at the right time. You arrange the circumstances in your favor and increase the chances of meeting the kind of people who can be of value to you, and you to them. Where there are people, there is potential. So put yourself around as many of the "right" ones as possible. Consider the following scenarios:

If you are at a restaurant that has individual tables and a larger community one, sit at the community one. There is a chance you will find yourself sitting next to someone who changes your life. I did this very thing the other day and ended up being joined by a group of women from one of the largest multilevel networking organizations in the country who were in town for a convention. They will be looking for a keynote speaker next year, and you can be certain I will do everything I can to make sure it's me.

If you find yourself on an elevator and have the option to take it alone or hold the door so someone else can join you, hold the door. Yes, because it's polite. And yes, because you may very well be traveling up or down with someone who can expand your business, your career, your income, or your life. I did it a few months ago and ended up sharing the elevator with someone who runs a hundred-million-dollar division of a consumer products company. We have spoken and exchanged a few e-mails since and are trying to find a time when we can get together again so that I can make a presentation about my services.

If you are taking a taxi and have the opportunity to share it with someone, do so. The last time I did that I drove into town with the guy who runs the entire strategy practice for the second largest consulting firm in the world.

If you are walking to a meeting room at a convention and can take a direct path or take a longer route that allows you to run into some people, take the long way.

If you always stand at the same place on the sidelines of the soccer field to watch your kids play, stand somewhere different once in a while. These people to whom you put yourself in proximity might very well end up representing the biggest opportunity of your lifetime.

Of course, arranging the circumstances isn't just about being around as many people as you can; it's about being around the *right kinds* of people. I try to get upgraded to first class when I travel by air as often as possible, because that's where the senior execs are. My fiancé, a wedding planner and floral designer, makes a point of wandering through the bridal magazine section in the bookstore, striking up conversations with women who are flipping through bridal magazines. After all, they're perfect prospects for her business. If you are a personal trainer, you would be wise to hang around from time to time in the nutritional supplement section of the supermarket.

There are always different ways to get where you're going, and there will always be those new paths presented to you—the ones that don't seem familiar or that don't naturally attract you. But if you want to expand your contact base through random networking, you must take, as Robert Frost did, "the road not taken."

During a recent trip to Narita, Japan, I took the hotel shuttle bus to a section of town that foreigners don't typically visit. During the ride, I struck up a conversation with another hotel guest who turned out to be a director of operations for a large Asian shipping company. Only he and I were on the bus, and I could've kept to myself and avoided making conversation. But instead, I made a point of initiating conversation while en route, and because of that, I learned about his company, his marketplace, his competitors, and his sales force—all of which expanded my knowledge base and got me thinking about an Asian marketing strategy.

I often take the longest route possible when I travel, simply for the purpose of giving myself increased chances to meet more people. I recently flew to Seattle from Atlanta; although I could have taken a direct flight, I instead booked the trip through New York, then Minneapolis. This gave me two extra legs during which I could meet potential leads; I guess you'd say, making more connections to make more connections. And make them I did. On the first leg, I met a woman who runs a division of a multinational human resources consulting firm. We're having lunch next week. On the second leg, I sat next to someone who started out as a long-shot random networking prospect—a college student. But I discovered over the course of our discussion that his school has what he considers a weak career placement department, so I plan to call the director to discuss how my company might be of assistance. I fully expect to turn at least one of these contacts into a profitable business relationship.

To expand your universe of possibilities and discover new opportunities, there are a number of "usual spots" you can vary:

- Restaurants
- Coffee shops
- Supermarkets
- Dry cleaners
- Transportation routes and modes
- Seating assignments

- Industry events
- Hotels
- Bank branches
- Car washes (yes, you can make random connections at car washes)
- Bookstores
- Anywhere else you are likely to find those who are in need of your products, services, or capabilities

When it comes to random networking, turning uncertainty into opportunity is the name of the game. Make meeting new people a goal. Decide you will meet someone new every day and create the space in your daily activities for putting yourself where others are.

Chapter at a Glance

- We have to fight our natural tendency to do the same thing the same way in the same places.
- Put yourself in new situations where you will have the chance to meet new people.
- Take the road less traveled, even if it makes the journey a little longer.

4

Schmooze or Lose

Many people believe that success in business is based solely on numbers and money or that success in life is about focus, discipline, and goal attainment. Although these formulas are valid to a degree, there is an overarching ingredient that trumps all others: it's called people. If you want to be successful in business or in life, you have to be successful with people. You have to be able to connect with people from different walks of life, and with all kinds of personalities and communication styles. You have to know how to build relationships. You must share a little bit of yourself in exchange for others sharing a little bit of *themselves*. This builds relationship equity—trust, mutual respect, likability. And it creates access to unlimited opportunity.

There's a saying that "nothing happens until somebody says something." Progress simply isn't made when people don't talk to one another. Information doesn't flow, ideas aren't exchanged, and energy doesn't move. But when one party opens his or her mouth and speaks up, conversation starts, thoughts are shared, creativity comes alive, possibilities appear, and the world—both yours and theirs—changes . . . usually for the better.

The way we get to know someone and build a relationship is through talking—good old-fashioned conversation. The Yiddish word *schmooze* means "to chat, to converse, to talk." Some call it shooting the breeze, and others refer to it as chewing the fat. But at the end of the day, it pretty much all means the same thing: two people sharing thoughts, feelings, and observations through conversation, all for the sake of getting to know each other.

In random connecting, it's simply a matter of opening your mouth and saying something to the person next to you, in front of you, behind you, or across from you. It doesn't have to be a declaration of deep and lasting consequence; it can be a comment about what's happening around you, a question, or even a statement that welcomes a response. Remarks about the weather have been triggering exchanges between people for centuries. Compliments almost always get a positive conversation started: "Love your shirt," "Love your shoes," "Love your watch," "Love your hair," or "Love your briefcase." Remarking in a positive way about someone, or something he or she has with them, is a sure way to initiate a favorable conversation with a stranger. It shows the other person that you are generous with your outlook, it makes that person feel good, and it provides a launching pad for further conversation.

These days, many of us are engaged in some form of personal technology when we're in public places. And most of us are still discovering how we feel about these particular items and how well they work for us. So a question about how the other person likes his or her smartphone, iPad, Bluetooth, or whatever else he or she may be interacting with is sure to trigger getting a conversation going. And it will break the spell of technology that can so easily engross us. Then it's simply a matter of listening, watching, asking, responding, sharing, nodding, expounding, laughing, and talking— in a word, *schmoozing*.

CASE STUDY: Jerry Z. schmoozes with a stranger at the gas station and finds his way to a new business partnership.

A sales manager at a luxury car dealership outside Atlanta, Jerry opened his mouth and schmoozed his way into an international business partnership. His random encounter occurred when he sparked a conversation with a complete stranger while pumping gas on his way home from work. As Jerry tells the story:

I was working for a Mercedes dealer at the time and stopped to fill up at a gas station I don't usually use. While standing there I noticed the man at the next pump filling a new Mercedes E-Class.

As a lover of fine automobiles, and always on the lookout for a prospective customer, I leaned between the pumps and asked him, "So how do you like your Mercedes?" We easily fell into a chat about cars, and I mentioned that I worked for a dealer. He seemed interested in that information, so we exchanged business cards almost immediately.

We continued talking—about cars, about business in general, and ultimately, about our respective work lives. I asked him about his company, and listened intently to his responses, showing a sincere interest in what he was saying. (I learned later that he was struck by how easily and naturally I engaged him in conversation.) I also talked about some of my career interests, beyond selling cars. Finally, he looked me in the eye, and asked, "Jerry, what is it you *really* want to do with your career?"

I replied that I had really always wanted to get into the import/export business. My father was from Palestine and my mother from Colombia, so I grew up speaking both

(continued)

Arabic and Spanish, along with English. My whole outlook on life was international.

I learned my new connection also had an international orientation. And, would you believe, he ran an import/export company! We kept talking, and he explained that the key to success in that business was in making connections and building trust. He told me that he admired my ability to talk to people. I asked if I could phone him to continue learning about his company and explore possibilities for us to do something together.

As we interacted over the following weeks and months via phone conversations and e-mails, I began to learn the language of the import/export business. My new connection taught me how deals were structured and that striking these deals took especially good relationship skills. Finally, he asked me one day if I would work with him on an import opportunity. Of course I said yes; and together we completed a deal that led to a lucrative financial reward for both of us. And it all began with a simple question to the man at the pump next to me: "So how do you like your Mercedes?"— and a little schmoozing about cars and business.

Chapter at a Glance

- Success in life requires success with people.
- Conversation builds relationships.
- When we talk with others, energy flows and new possibilities are created.

5

The Limits of Online Connections

The Internet and social media have presented new and seemingly unlimited opportunities for expanding our networks. Facebook, LinkedIn, Twitter, not to mention all the online tools yet to be invented, are in many ways redefining the way we interact and socialize. With the push of a button, you can add dozens, even hundreds, of names to your contact base. And for sure, those names represent opportunities you can uncover—some directly; some indirectly. Yet nothing will ever beat sharing physical space, shaking a hand, and looking someone in the eye when it comes to creating and cultivating quality relationships. As Warren Buffet, the icon of business and investor success, asks in his ad for the National Business Aviation Association, "Ever give a firm handshake over a speakerphone?" He would likely ask the same question in the context of the Internet.

For better or worse, depending on your perspective, Facebook has redefined the word *friend*, and LinkedIn has recast the word *connection*. To me, a friend is someone who will be there for you any time, all the time, someone who knows you well and whom *you* know. There is a level of trust that permeates a friendship. You have a history with a friend, where time and personal sharing build mutual experiences that form the foundation of the relationship.

LinkedIn has made connections a numbers game, sometimes with little regard for relevance, influence, or the quality of the contact. It's a contest for how many people you can add to your connections, rather than their likelihood of actually helping you in some way, or their degree of influence, authority, and resources.

Although useful in their own way, online connections don't give you the richness of face-to-face communication, and the absence of in-person chemistry limits the quality of your interaction. When we're online, we frequently find ourselves in a relationship with a screen instead of a person. In fact, the Internet makes it all too easy to form "phony" connections. If you don't believe that, consider this: I recently met someone who told me he created a Facebook page for an imaginary person. He made up the name and invented activities and interests, the birthday, photos, walls, and pokes. Then he put out friend requests. At last count he had over 100 acceptances. These people accepted a friend request from a person who didn't even exist! Some people have thousands of LinkedIn connections, most of whom they have never met or spoken to, and probably never will.

Of course, I network online, as should anyone who wants to build his or her business or personal brand. I reach out to people over the Internet. I have relationships with people I contact solely via the phone. I, too, have associates and colleagues I've never laid eyes on. But it is the individuals I've met in person—in the most random ways and most unlikely places—who have broadened my knowledge, expanded my network, enriched my life, and increased my bank account well beyond what would have been had I merely connected with them online.

There is no better way to create credibility for yourself or your products, services, or capabilities than by sharing physical, in-the-moment space with someone. Putting a face with a name and experiencing the magic of in-person interaction establishes credibility and allows us to forge relationships faster and with more lasting power than is possible through the click of a mouse.

To be fair, online networking is incredibly powerful. It can expand your pool of contacts quickly and broadly, and it's highly efficient for reaching across a wide swath of the marketplace. It can add names to your contact list you wouldn't be able to add solely on your own. Yet more often than not, web-based connections require that you have a face-to-face encounter at some point in order to manifest in a profitable business relationship. You can answer a job posting online, but eventually you will have to attend an interview. You can present your products and services via a website or webinar, but no prospect is going to spend big money with you until he or she meets you in person. You can position your professional services via a social networking platform, but you won't be doing consulting for a company until you meet the client in the flesh. And prospects might find you and your business on the web, but chances are they won't let you list their house, prepare their taxes, or tutor their children until they look you in the eye and gain the comfort that comes from face-to-face communication.

Chapter at a Glance

- The Internet has redefined the concepts of connection and friend.
- Online personas are easy to fake.
- Online connections don't necessarily translate into productive or profitable relationships.
- Shaking a hand and looking someone in the eye is one of the highest quality forms of communication.

6

When Traditional Networking Is *Not* Working

Over the last 10 years, and especially in the past 5, formalized networking events have become a popular venue for professionals to meet and interact—and they, too, have their place in the networking recipe. But while community and industry gatherings can attract a lot of people, they don't necessarily attract the right people, that is, the ones who'll do you the most good. Buyers, or those in positions of influence, don't always attend. In fact, they occasionally make a point of *purposely* staying away. Networking events attract sellers, and there is only one thing worse than a room full of sellers with no buyers, and that's a room full of sellers with only a handful of buyers.

In fact, the people you find in coffee shops, at restaurants, in bars, at airports, on airplanes, at sporting events, and at social gatherings represent even more potential, because you are more than likely meeting them when they are most relaxed, accessible, and most available—in short, when they are most themselves. In a traditional networking setting, people are apt to be barraging your potential contact with demands for his or her attention. Individuals, especially those in a position of power, tend to erect a wall of sorts when they know that others will be approaching and asking for something. However, when you meet these same people outside the framework of traditional networking, you often find them at their most unguarded and mentally and emotionally available moments.

CASE STUDY: A random encounter in a doctor's office leads to a new supplier—and the perfect prescription for saving money on a marketing project for Isabel A.

As Isabel tells it:

> Random connecting goes both ways between sellers and buyers. I met a supplier in a physician's waiting room who helped me through a difficult budgetary challenge at work.
>
> I was managing a major direct-mail program involving more than 1 million customers. My management had just cut my budget in half but required me to generate the same results. I really did not know what to do, but a medical appointment turned out to be just what the doctor ordered!
>
> A doctor's office is the least likely place I would have thought to make a business connection, but sitting in the waiting room, I noticed another woman across from me. We began talking about our respective conditions and how we found this particular doctor.
>
> As part of this getting-to-know-you conversation, we started talking about what we do for a living. Imagine my delight when she said her company did direct-mail print production. I think she was equally delighted when I told her I had a need for exactly those kinds of services.

When it was her turn to see the doctor, we exchanged business cards and I promised to call. When we spoke the next day, I gave her the spec for the job I needed to get done and she gave me pricing that enabled me to get my project completed within the new budget limitations.

Within a month she had her first order from me. We did business for a number of years, and she continued to offer money-saving suggestions that made me and my boss very happy. We also became good friends, going to concerts and art shows together. Meeting her reminded me that you never know who you're going to meet, wherever you are!

With the exception of conventions and industry conferences, people in positions of influence tend to stay away from places where they are going to be captured, bound, and pitched. People with money, influence, access, and power know that they're targets for those who want some or all of those things. It's therefore not surprising that they don't tend to go out of their way to put themselves in venues where they'll encounter more of it.

Don't misunderstand; there *is* value in getting to know your fellow sellers. You can share company names, discuss insights on marketplace activity, exchange business cards, and talk about each other's work. And even sellers are sometimes buyers. At the end of the day, though, you are more likely to meet people similar to you at industry or community networking events—sellers trying to meet people who have the authority to buy or who can influence those who do.

However, if you are trying to find qualified leads, you won't find the best of them at networking events. The real action is in a coffee shop, in a copy shop, in a hair salon, on the sidelines of a high school soccer field, in an office building elevator, or in the waiting room of the car dealership.

Chapter at a Glance

- Traditional networking events tend to attract people searching for influence, not those who have it.
- There is no bad networking, just some that's more fruitful than others.
- The real action is often in the places you least expect to find it.

Face It: Nothing Beats the Chemistry of In-Person Communication

As the world goes digital and relationships are increasingly available with the click of a mouse, the opportunities for face-to-face interaction seem to be waning. But that very reason is what makes the value of in-person communication even greater.

In a society that increasingly exists on the Internet, the impact and importance of in-person communication has given way to keyboards, wireless routers, computer screens, and pixels. Most young people don't think of personal contact first as a way to build relationships. They would be more likely to tweet or "friend." Yet face-to-face, in-person communication is the richest, most complete form of interaction two people can have. It's better than a phone conversation, better than an e-mail exchange, and better than a text message, a tweet, a LinkedIn in-message, or Facebook friend request.

We've all had the experience of communicating with someone via e-mail, text, or phone, sometimes even over an extended period of time, where we create a visual picture of the person and their personality. Sometimes we even *have* a picture of them. We might think we really know them. Then we meet in person, and WOW—we get a whole new perspective when we're finally in their physical presence.

Call it chemistry. Call it an energy field or a vibe. But whatever you call it, you surely know what it is. And you no doubt experience it in your everyday life. It's what motivates you to get together with someone when you have something important to discuss. It's what causes you to want to meet with someone in person when you really want to get to know him or her. Just seeing the person is not enough, as anyone who has videoconferenced or used Skype can attest. Admittedly, seeing someone via video is better than only hearing the person's voice, and generally better than interacting in writing. However, if you've ever met someone in person *after* having a video or Skype exchange, you realize the power of in-person chemistry.

Unfortunately, this growing emphasis on social networking means that a lot of people are missing the chance to make high-quality connections and form solid relationships. And as fewer people practice face-to-face networking, they also lose the chance to hone the skills that it requires. Some people are more introverted than others: they don't like to reach out to complete strangers. It's intimidating, awkward, unfamiliar, and threatening to them. Yet as with any skill, the more you practice it, the easier it gets—and the better you become at it. Making a point of talking to strangers, building rapport with new connections, and cultivating face-to-face relationships will strengthen your ability to do so. Shaking someone's hand, looking that person in the eyes, sharing physical space, and exchanging mutually respectful conversation will become more comfortable and enriching every time you do these things.

In-person communication is packed with information about the other person and what makes him or her tick. Your ability to observe and gauge the other person's responses can tell you how he or she really feels and what he or she truly thinks. Unlike online networking, face-to-face interaction provides more—and more fruitful—information. Being in someone's presence lets you look into that person's eyes, watch physical movements, and hear the subtleties of the voice. And although you can pick up voice clues on the phone, in-person communication offers a complete "information package." You can witness the other person's body language and reactions to what you say. You can discern subtle changes in skin tone and breathing patterns, as well as an entire range of information signals that are available only in face-to-face communication. You can more easily discern the impact that your communication is having when the other party's eyes dart away based on something you just said. When someone takes a deep breath (which *is* noticeable on the phone but not as easily recognized when you're in person), you gain insight into how that person is reacting. When someone shifts his or her body posture in response to something you say, you pick up valuable clues about the content of your conversation and the effect you are having.

You assess much of this information about others—information that lets us know who they are, what they think, how they *really* feel—on an unconscious level. Our brains are able to ascertain large amounts of data on levels of which we are not even aware. But you have to be in the other person's physical space to recognize it.

Bottom line: when it comes to making valuable business connections and leveraging them into mutually profitable relationships, the money's in the face-to-face meeting. With only few exceptions, if someone is going to hire you, he or she is going to want to meet you in person, even if you've previously met on a video chat. If an investor is going to plunk down hard-earned money into your company, he or she is going to want to get together with you in the flesh, probably a number of times. If someone is going to buy your product or service, he or she is going to want more than just having you as a name in his or her LinkedIn connections. All of these people are going to want to see you, feel you (well, sort of), and gain those subtle insights about you—clues that come through only in in-person, face-to-face interactions.

Chapter at a Glance

- Face-to-face interaction is the richest, most meaningful interaction two people can have.
- Even videoconferencing doesn't convey the fullness of one's personality and character.
- When we are in someone else's physical presence, there is a chemistry that deepens connection.
- Important business deals almost always require an in-person meeting.

8

Anonymity—A Random Connector's Greatest Advantage

Lest you think strangers are less willing to share information, think again. They're very often *more* forthright, as counterintuitive as this may seem. Anonymity actually works to your advantage during a random encounter, because people are surprisingly more eager to share facts about themselves with someone they don't know than with people they do. They simply assume they'll never see or hear from you again, and until names are exchanged, you're still a complete stranger. And that means you're safe. They will therefore tell you things they would never tell someone who came to see them in their office and give you information they'd never give a colleague. But they'll share it with you because, after all, it's all under the veil of anonymity—and as far as they know, it will continue to be.

In the first few moments of a random exchange, you don't know the other person and he or she doesn't know you. It's safe. It's comfortable. In these situations, you can find out a great deal about others—what they do for a living, what company they work for, even where they live, where they're from, and where they're going. You might even find out what's important to them, whether they're happy with their life circumstances, and what they do and don't like about their work, home, company, and more.

Under the shared veil of anonymity, you can offer up bits and pieces of your life, too, so all is fair. You're not building a dossier; you're merely exchanging information about yourself with each other without feeling threatened or invaded. The level of comfort and trust remains as you continue in conversation and lob back and forth even more information. Yet you still don't know each other's names.

Then comes a time to actually "meet." The hand goes out for shaking, along with "My name is…" In that moment the conversation shifts to another plane. By this point you have already shared information in both directions and established trust, and the possibilities for the relationship begin to come into view.

From here, with the foundation in place, you can take the conversation to the next level, exploring and discovering what is possible between you. So much for believing that people won't share information with strangers!

Chapter at a Glance

- People are more likely to share information about themselves when they are anonymous.
- You can gain a lot of insight about someone before you even introduce yourself.
- Once the information is shared, you have a solid foundation for expanding the relationship.

9

We're All Connected

Whatever it is that you want—a new client, a better job or career, a business of your own, more money, a wider social circle—you can't get it alone. No one can. We need each other to achieve our goals and dreams. Howard Schultz didn't make Starbucks into a global coffee company all by himself. Jack Welch didn't make GE one of the most valuable companies in the history of American business sitting alone in his office. Oprah Winfrey didn't become "Oprah" single-handedly. They all needed others to make it happen. They may get all the glory (and take all the credit), but their list of acknowledgments is no doubt deep and long.

That's why random networking works. It always has been, and always will be, through others that we achieve our objectives and realize our hopes. That's the power of synchronicity. You need something, and presto, it shows up in the person sitting next to you. There's something someone else needs, and poof, there you are for him or her.

Synchronicity is the reason this book is in your hands right now. About a year ago I was sitting next to someone on a flight, a complete stranger who was deeply immersed in a spiral-bound notebook.

He was reading intensely and making notes, occasionally staring up in thought, and then adding sentences and commentary to the pages. *What is he working on?* I wondered. *A business plan? A brochure? A presentation?* I didn't want to interrupt his concentration, so I knew I would have to wait for the right moment to initiate conversation. So when he took a break from his intense focus, I seized the moment. "Wow, that looks like a pretty intense project you're working on," I said in an empathetic and respectful way, to show that I know what it's like to be immersed in an intensely creative project.

Well, indeed it was. This man turned out to be an author with two cookbooks to his credit who was planning a strategy for his newest restaurant. Nothing could have been more relevant—and no one could have been more valuable—to me in that moment than an author who had connections with book publishers. I had been looking for a literary expert to represent and advise me on my book, and I wasn't sure how to proceed.

"You could call my agent," he said. "And tell her I suggested you get in touch. She's one of the best—and delightful to work with," he added. I did call her as soon as I got home, and indeed she guided, coached, and represented me.

Synchronicity emerged again months later. I was at a copy shop in midtown Manhattan and struck up a conversation with a woman who was printing what appeared to be a manuscript. "Looks like you might be writing a book," I remarked.

"Sure am, in between waitressing and recording music," she said.

"How exciting!" I replied. "What's the topic, and how's it going?" I asked.

"Well, it's for young adults, and it's going fine, except I just need to find an agent to help me get it published."

Needless to say, I was delighted to provide one for her, and that random encounter gave this woman what may very well be the biggest opportunity of her lifetime, not to mention a book that may enhance the lives of hundreds of thousands of teens around the world. All this was possible because of synchronicity and the willingness to pierce the veil of autonomy and talk to a stranger.

We are far more dependent on each other than we even realize. Did you accomplish *your* greatest achievements by yourself? How many others contributed to or influenced your success, either directly or indirectly? Go so far as to think back to your childhood; didn't your teachers, friends, friends' parents, coaches, or maybe a boss or mentor help you in some way?

If you still don't believe that you need others to achieve your goals and dreams, you won't be inclined to reach out to them— in random encounters or otherwise. And you will sadly miss the opportunities that surround you every day. It is in most people's natures to want to help others. It gives us a sense of purpose and of accomplishment. It just feels good. Helping each other is what makes the world go 'round.

CASE STUDY: Synchronicity turned a leisurely cigar conversation at a downtown Chicago smoking lounge into a major business deal for Andy T. and Jim N.

As Jim tells it:

> Nearly a year ago, my business partner was enjoying a cigar at a downtown Chicago cigar store and smoking lounge— an ideal setting for conversation on any subject you may imagine. He began chatting with a fellow smoker, a complete stranger, sharing opinions about their favorite cigars, where they buy them, and where they smoke them. After building some rapport, the conversation eventually turned to business, and the fellow cigar smoker found my partner's business intriguing. He suggested my partner call a colleague of his named Fred who might be very interested in learning more about our company. He gave my partner Fred's phone number, and my partner turned it over to me for follow-up.

(continued)

Not wanting to pass up a potential business opportunity, I called Fred who—as it turns out—was a senior vice president at a major supermarket chain with stores across the United States and Europe. His company would be a great target for our product. I learned about a new potential customer and was introduced to other decision makers in Fred's organization. Had we made that connection only through the introduction by the fellow cigar smoker, it would have been a great story. However, Fred was just about to leave his position with the supermarket chain and was going to launch his own business. We worked with him on his business plan, but he was offered a senior job at another supermarket chain just as he was about to launch it. In the interim, Fred had introduced us to his business partner for the company he was going to start, who also had contacts at leading supermarkets throughout the world. As it turned out, Fred took the new job and will hopefully become a customer. But his business partner has joined forces with our company and is selling our products to customers across the country. None of this would've happened had it not been for the chance encounter that my partner had with a fellow cigar smoker on the North Shore of Chicago. You just never know who will be on the other end of that first handshake with a stranger and where it will lead.

Chapter at a Glance

- We need each other to achieve our goals and dreams; we can't do it alone.
- Even those who get the credit for creating great things will ultimately admit they needed others to make it happen.
- It is human nature to want to help others.
- When we help one another, we tap into the magic of synchronicity.

10

The Four Beliefs of Successful Random Connectors

Although successful random connecting takes practice and skill, it requires something even more essential: a positive, can-do attitude. After all, here you are presenting yourself to the world at large, engaging complete strangers in meaningful conversation, asking them to trust you enough to sometimes share personal information, and essentially breaking through the walls most people put around them in public places. So nothing is more important than your state of mind and belief system about the world around you and your place in it. Our beliefs drive our behavior; when you truly believe something is possible—and that *you* can make it happen—you are far more likely to prove yourself right. As such, the following four beliefs are all you need to have the confidence for turning random encounters into potentially life-changing relationships.

You may already accept some of these tenets to one degree or another, whereas some others may take a small leap of faith. But when you believe them in your bones, and live them fully, you will find opportunities opening up to you in ways you never knew were possible.

1. The World Is a Friendly Place

Even in today's world where governments jockey for dominance and wars are being fought on many continents, there is a commonality among human beings that makes random connecting possible. Wherever you travel—across nations, cultures, societies, races, creeds, and colors—you will find that everyone has a common set of desires: to be acknowledged, understood, respected, and appreciated. Almost everyone around the globe appreciates a hot meal, a good night's sleep, the innocence of a child, a funny joke, or a good story. And right below the surface, just about everyone has a smile, a chuckle, a willingness to meet you halfway, and a desire to help a fellow human being. That's because many of us face similar challenges, struggle with similar issues, and desire similar things. You smile, and other people smile. You shrug; they shrug. You just can't get away from it.

To be a successful random connector, you must trust first and foremost—from the moment you leave your house each day—that the world is a friendly place. After all, if you don't believe that the world is friendly, you won't reach out to strangers and will instead be withdrawn and isolated. But by assuming people are fundamentally friendly, your attitude will operate in a way that gives you the confidence to approach others and allow you to discover all that's possible from your new random encounter.

There is a commonality of experience that just about everyone can relate to. It's the thread of humanity that connects us as human beings. Everywhere I've ever been around the world, across cultures, ages, races, and income levels, I have found that almost everyone:

- Likes ice cream and chocolate chip cookies.
- Thinks kids are cute (and are proud of their own).

- Wants a good night's sleep.
- Will laugh at a good joke.
- Loves a good story (especially when the underdog comes out on top).
- Hates waiting in line and appreciates good customer service.
- Enjoys a warm meal.
- Seeks to be loved, acknowledged, understood, and appreciated.
- Wants more from life.
- Is looking for human connection.

These are among the common threads of human existence that give us connecting points with other people and turn strangers into associates, colleagues, partners, and friends. It's how we penetrate the veil of isolation that threatens to limit our lives, and open up a world of opportunity. It's how we get a smile, a running start on a great conversation, and potential that exceeds our wildest imagination.

2. Everyone Can Be Met

What you believe is possible has everything to do with what you make happen. There are some who believe that strangers are meant to stay that way, that people aren't really available, don't want to be bothered, and are shut down, shut off, and inaccessible. And since our beliefs precede our behavior—and therefore, our results—those who believe that people are not open or available find that people *aren't* open or available. They create their own reality. They fail to make eye contact with strangers or pay attention to what others are doing. They surely don't strike up conversations about a shared experience in the moment. And as a result, they also probably have a small and stagnant base of contacts, with an opportunity pipeline that trickles rather than gushes. And their options for personal, professional, and financial growth are probably limited.

Successful random connectors, on the other hand, firmly believe that just about anyone can be met—that if approached appropriately and respectfully, most people are willing to connect with others.

Think about the times when you have made a connection with a stranger; you will realize that just below the surface, the person was quite open and willing.

Have you ever made a lighthearted comment to a stranger and had the person scowl at you? Have you ever made a remark to someone you didn't know in an effort to befriend him or her only to be completely ignored? Most people who are out and about in public places—whether attending business meetings, shopping in malls, or traveling on trains or planes—find that only a thin veneer exists between their outer shell and a receptive response. Everyone has a smile, a laugh, or even a mutual sentiment waiting just below the surface that can be shared in that split second of common human experience.

You can meet just about anyone, literally. Even if the person is sitting three rows up from you, standing 20 feet away from you, leaving a place as you're arriving, arriving as you're leaving, or talking intensely on his or her cell phone—all you have to do is put yourself in physical proximity to that person, wait for the appropriate moment, and say something engaging.

People are often more accessible than they appear, so just because they don't look like they're waiting to meet you, they very well may be underneath. After all, most people don't wear a sign on their head saying "Please talk to me! I can be your next customer or maybe help you find a better job." But if you approach them gently, respectfully, and with curiosity, you may very well find that's exactly the case. Believe you can meet anyone you want—and you can and will.

3. Almost Everyone You Meet Can Enhance Your Life in Some Way

There is value to just about every relationship you create, even if it isn't obvious at the beginning. This core assumption is what drives random networking success: the belief that everyone has, in some way or another, something to offer. The possibilities can go in many directions, and you won't even know what they are until you initiate and become involved in these conversations.

The entire planet is one big people portal. It's a pathway to revenue, career opportunities, information of all sorts, or at the very least, a social connection. The value of these random connections can come directly from the connections themselves, the people they know in their professional spheres of influence, or their relatives and/or friends.

If you are in the business of selling something, you can find potential clients through random encounters. If you are unemployed or dissatisfied in your job, the people you meet out and about can hire you or direct you to people or companies that can. If you have a successful career and want to stay current, you may discover something new that gives you a professional or competitive advantage. Or you might find a friend you keep for a lifetime.

Your ability to uncover opportunities by making new and chance connections depends on the way in which you think about the world around you. The world will manifest opportunities to you in direct proportion to how much opportunity you believe is there for the taking. So believe that a world of possibility awaits you every day—and it will.

4. You Can Enhance the Life of Everyone You Meet

The fourth and final belief of successful random networkers is the knowledge that you have value to others who will ultimately drive your success. Random connecting isn't just about what others can do for you; it's about what you can bring to them, too. And no matter what you do for a living or where you are in your life, you always have some kind of value to offer. It might come from the company you represent, the products you sell, the services you provide, your subject matter knowledge in your area of expertise, your insights, and all that you can offer others from your portfolio of professional and personal experiences.

People are going to buy what you offer only if those things make a positive difference to them. They are going to contract for your services only if you somehow will improve their life or circumstances. And people are going to be far more inclined to share high-quality information with you—the kind that expands your life—if you share some quality information with them.

You are worthy of others' time and attention. You have the ability to change their lives for the better, but only if you believe you can.

Knowing and living this fourth belief will give you the confidence to reach out to others, in any place and under any circumstance. You are worthy of every random encounter you make—and the connection that follows—by virtue of what you bring, what you know, what you do, and just who you are.

How you think about the world around you and the people in it makes all the difference in your ability to expand your life through making random connections and turning strangers into productive relationships. In Table 10.1, notice the difference between the two columns and how much more opportunity there will be for you when you embrace the beliefs that expand your possibilities.

Do you want more clients? Would you like to gain a competitive advantage in your industry? Build partnerships and alliances for your business? Have an investor in your company? Explore a different career direction? Find a new job? You can define your goals, write a business plan, and map a strategy, but at the end of the day you will need people to help make it happen.

It always has been, and always will be, through who we know that we achieve our goals, realize our dreams, and expand our lives. And although the advent of social media provides a fabulous new channel for meeting and communicating with people, if you want connections that turn into productive business relationships, you are likely to find them in your daily travels, every day, all day long.

The world is a friendly place, and you can meet anyone, finding customers, partners, investors, mentors, and friends, simply by

Table 10.1 What You Believe Is Directly Related to What You Achieve

Beliefs That Will *Limit* You From Expanding Your Life	Beliefs That Will *Enable* You to Expand Your Life
The world is not a friendly place.	The world *is* a friendly place.
I don't have anything worthwhile to offer.	My product, service, or subject matter knowledge is valuable to others.
If I am not sitting or standing near the other person, it's impossible to connect.	I can maneuver my way to be close enough to initiate a conversation.
People don't want to be bothered.	People are social creatures and hungry for human connection.
That person probably isn't worth meeting.	Everyone has something worthwhile to offer, and I just don't know what it is yet.
People don't like to talk about themselves.	People like it when someone else shows interest in them.
I don't know what to say to initiate the conversation.	There are dozens of observations I can make, insights I can share, or questions I can ask that will create a conversation path.
Others will think I'm weird if I just start talking to them.	People will open up and respond favorably if I approach them respectfully by showing curiosity and genuine interest.
He doesn't look friendly.	People don't always look like what or who they are, and the only way I'll know is if I make a friendly comment.

(*continued*)

Table 10.1   Continued

Beliefs That Will *Limit* You From Expanding Your Life	Beliefs That Will *Enable* You to Expand Your Life
She (or he) might think I am hitting on her (or him).	If I keep the conversation on purely professional terms, she (or he) will not misconstrue my intention.
I am not a desirable job candidate.	My background and experience make me a valuable contributor wherever I work.
If I try to sell this person something, he or she will resent it.	What I offer makes others' lives better, so he or she is likely to be glad I made it available.

talking to strangers. You are just a comment, a question, a remark, or a compliment away from tapping unlimited potential. In the next section you will discover the key principles and techniques for turning your everyday random encounters into meaningful and productive relationships.

Chapter at a Glance

- Your attitude and beliefs about what is possible will drive your ability to make great things happen.
- If you believe that people are friendly and receptive to meeting you, you will find that they are.
- When you believe everyone can enhance your life in some way and you can enhance theirs, you will bring a whole new dimension to the encounters you have every day.

SECTION

II

Turning Random Encounters Into Mutually Beneficial Relationships

The ability to have successful random encounters begins with your thought process and attitude. As we discussed in the previous section, if you believe you can meet anyone—that people are fundamentally friendly and that you, and everyone you meet, has something worthwhile to offer—then you will increase your chances of making an endless number of valuable contacts in your daily life.

Yet random connecting is also a *skill*, one that requires specific strategies and tactics to implement successfully. And although it's not difficult, it's like any other skill in that it entails focus and discipline. You probably already have some of the skills required to make productive face-to-face associations, whereas others might be new. In either case, this section will show you how to learn, build, and/or sharpen these proficiencies so that you can turn everyday random encounters into mutually profitable relationships.

11

Find Clues to Initiate Conversation

The entire random encounter process begins with your ability to initiate conversation with a complete stranger. For many of us, the biggest challenge is knowing where to begin. What should you talk about? How do you find that point of entry into the conversation? And *whom* should you talk to, given a room, airplane, lobby, or elevator full of people?

In the 1960s and 1970s, people placed bumper stickers on their cars to make a statement or indicate something about their circumstances, personalities, or values. Sometimes they were funny, sometimes political, sometimes very personal. In all cases, they gave insights into people, their beliefs, their likes and dislikes, and what they considered important. Thirty and forty years ago, bumper stickers said things like "Let's All Do the Twist," "Hug a Hippie," "Peace and Love," or "Nixon in '60." These were literally and figuratively signs of the times that indicated car owners' personal and political inclinations.

Today's bumper stickers say things like "Driver Carries No Cash...He's Married," "Four Out of Three People Have Trouble with Fractions," or "Guns Don't Kill People; Drivers With Cell Phones Do." Like those of the 1960s, these give insights into a person's sense of humor, interests, priorities, and even values. If you pulled up beside someone with any of these on their bumper, you would have a clue about the person, and maybe even be able to say something about their statement that resonates with them.

Although the popularity of bumper stickers has come and gone, the good news is that people often provide information about themselves in other subtle ways—through the clothes they wear, the things they carry, and what they're doing. In these items, you can find little pieces of information that people give out about themselves, either directly or indirectly. These little gems are the golden keys for random connectors, because they unlock content you can use for initiating conversation.

The following are some ways people broadcast information about themselves that you can use to initiate and direct your conversation:

- Luggage tag with laminated business card
- Clothing with embroidered company logo
- Backpack with embossed industry affiliation or conference
- Jewelry (rings, watches, bracelets) with award, achievement insignia, or college/university affiliation
- Lapel pins with logo, flag, or other insignia
- Binder with company logo
- Pens with logo or industry identification
- Company identification on laptop cover or screen
- Magazine or book
- Conversations loud enough to overhear from more than a few feet away

I met someone who became one of the most significant business partners of my career simply by noticing his business card and using it as a conversation clue. I was building a comprehensive multimedia training program and needed some content expertise to enhance my own. The challenge was finding someone who had the right knowledge *and* life circumstances to be available to work on an independent contractor basis. It couldn't be someone with a full-time job; it had to be an independent consultant-type who had the time and freedom required for the project.

Weeks went by as I tapped my network for someone who would fit that profile with no luck—until one day when I least expected it, there it was. While waiting to board a puddle jumper to western North Carolina, I saw with my very own eyes exactly what would lead me directly to what I was looking for: a business card of someone who worked for the leading sales training and development company in the country, attached to a piece of luggage and obviously belonging to one of the passengers who was boarding the plane with me. Although I wasn't sure who it was, I knew I would find out. I scanned the faces of my fellow seatmates once I boarded the plane but couldn't make a definite determination. I would have to watch carefully when we landed to see who would retrieve that suitcase and make contact then.

I made a point of being among the first off the plane and positioned myself near where the bags would be placed on the tarmac. When the person who belonged to the bags with the business card grabbed his luggage, I gently and politely asked if he in fact worked for the company. Yes, he did. I immediately began a line of conversation that would help me determine whether he was a candidate for my project. We chatted about the company and his role, which led to a conversation about my endeavor and the opportunity that might await him.

We worked closely together over the next two years, developing and marketing a highly successful multimedia training program. It was a business relationship born out of a complete random encounter, the result of my noticing a business card, believing I could meet the person to whom those bags belonged, putting myself close enough to make contact, and initiating conversation with a simple question.

Someone you see in a public place, such as an airport, coffee shop, hotel lobby, or any of dozens of other public venues, is more than likely receptive to meeting (to some degree). In addition, most people telegraph—sometimes blatantly, sometimes subtly—information about their availability and themselves. Someone sitting in the back of the coffee shop is probably somewhat less open and available than the person who chooses to sit in the middle or toward the front. Likewise, someone who is hunched over their computer in the corner of the hotel lobby is likely less available than the person sitting on the sectional sofa where there is room for others to sit nearby. These are subtle yet significant clues about how available someone is, and they are important guides for you as you approach your potential new acquaintance.

Chapter at a Glance

- People telegraph information about themselves in indirect but clear ways.
- Notice logos on clothing or travel items and insignias on jewelry or technology.
- These clues are ideal for helping formulate relevant conversation starters.

12

Avoid Judging People From a Distance

We tend to evaluate others based on surface assessments of how they look, how they're dressed, or what they're doing. It's human nature to make up stories about people based on what truly amounts to superficial data. And because it is superficial, the formulas we use don't always hold up. We think to ourselves: That person doesn't look friendly because she's frowning instead of smiling. This person doesn't look like he's influential because he's wearing cutoffs and has a few days' growth on his face. Or that person probably isn't worth meeting because she just got out of an older model car.

Have you ever read *The Millionaire Next Door?* Thomas J. Stanley and William D. Danko's book lets us in on an important fact: most millionaires drive old cars. And most have never spent more than a few hundred dollars on a suit. And oh, by the way, some of the most successful entrepreneurs don't even bother to shave every day.

No doubt, we as random connectors are seeking those who represent the greatest potential for having a mutually beneficial relationship. But just as a priceless piece of sterling silver may not

appear so on the surface, a hugely valuable connection may be waiting for you at the bus stop, in the coach section of the airplane, or
in the share-a-taxi line at the hotel. So although your preliminary
assessment of another person may be right, it may also be wrong.
And making the wrong call about a potential connection could be
costly. It might cause you to miss out on making one of the most
valuable contacts of your lifetime, just because you presumed that
the woman standing in front of you in line at the coffee shop in a
running suit isn't the CEO of a company who happens to be on
vacation…or working from home that day.

Chapter at a Glance

- People don't always look like what or who they are.
- Making an assumption about someone could be very costly.
- Some of the most influential people are understated in terms
  of dress and attitude.

13

Don't Be Overeager

When you attempt to talk to someone in a public venue for the purpose of networking, the way in which you reach out has everything to do with the result you get. In other words, it's all about the approach, with the venue being an important consideration. If you are in a place where the other person has overtly or implicitly agreed to socialize or be met, then that person is fair game. It is mutually understood that the person is willing to engage, and you have permission to strike up a conversation. Since both parties know this, the other person is less likely to be guarded or feel that you are trespassing in his or her personal space. Trade shows, industry conferences, professional events, and parties are obviously networking bonanzas; most everyone is open and receptive to making new relationships. You might say they're "all-you-can-meet" buffets.

However, random connecting differs from these kinds of venues in that you are approaching people in places where the other party has not necessarily agreed to be met. This is where your approach becomes so essential. It is especially important to be cognizant of the creep factor—not *the other person's* creep factor, but *yours*. Although there is often some initial unease (even in traditional networking events) on the other person's part about whether approaching another person is legit, this concern is heightened in random connecting. You don't want to come on too strong; rather, you want to ease into the interaction. You wouldn't turn to someone at a coffee shop and say, "I know you're here to get a cup of java but I'm trying to find a job, so if you don't mind, may I ask where you work, what you do, and if you have any authority to hire?" Although that might work occasionally, it will *not* work most of the time. It's too bold, in your face—and too early in the conversation to pose those kinds of questions.

The first thing to do when approaching a complete stranger with whom you want to connect is to simply assess the situation and person. Does the person seem receptive? Has he or she smiled or somehow acknowledged you in a welcoming way? Did the person make a non-verbal gesture of receptivity? If so, and it feels right to say something, go for it. Break the ice with a comment or question that creates a pathway to conversation (see Chapter 14 for examples of these).

Here are some guidelines for gauging when and how to approach someone when making a random encounter...

When the other person...   *Approach freely*
Initiates a conversation with *you*
Makes eye contact/smiles/gestures
Is standing or sitting facing you
Is wearing or carrying something with company logo or other
    easy identification
Is not immersed in personal technology
Is talking to someone loudly enough that you can hear them
Is making him- or herself obvious (i.e., sitting in the center of
    the room or near most of the activity)

When the other person...   *Approach, but cautiously*
Is working on a laptop in a public place
Is talking on a cell phone in a public place
Is reading
Responds to your opening statement but doesn't keep the
    conversation going

When the other person…	*Avoid completely*
Is working on a laptop in a private place	
Is talking on a cell phone in a private place	
Avoids eye contact	
Is wearing headphones or eye covers	
Is under a blanket	

If you're not quite sure what to do or say, the best thing to do when you are within talking range might simply be to allow a moment or two to pass *without* saying anything. By *not* filling those few seconds with words, you dissolve the defensiveness that others sometimes have when strangers approach. Coming across as *too* eager to connect can seem intrusive and inhibit the interaction before it even begins. We all know from our own experience that nobody likes to feel like the person befriending us is too overeager. There's a lot to be said for subtlety, that is, allowing some space between the initial proximity and the first comment and between the first utterance and the next remark in the conversation thread. Sometimes a few seconds is all it takes.

Making a comfortable connection with a complete stranger is much like volleying in tennis; there is a serve and then a return. The person who is serving hits the ball gently across the net directly to the other person, so the receiver needn't work hard to return it. You can then gauge what kind of player you have on the other side of the court—and how motivated that person is to play—based on how the ball comes back across the net.

You want to come across as neutral when you're connecting randomly. You must exude a nonthreatening, friendly, and authentic air. You will want to be curious as well, first in general, then as a natural extension of the conversation, and ultimately about what this person does for a living. And after all, you are curious, since you are simply gathering information at this point. You don't know if this person is in between assignments with the Peace Corps, the CEO of a major corporation, a stay-at-home dad who hasn't worked outside the house in five years, or a full-time college student.

Even though your goal is to determine whether there is a basis for a continued relationship, no one likes to feel as if he or she is being used for influence or authority, especially by a presumed stranger. Therefore, your initial approach is paramount to random connecting success.

Although most people in public venues are available to some degree and can be met, you must still be sensitive to people's situations. People give clues about how available they are; sometimes those clues are obvious and sometimes, less so. But the clues are there, and effective random connectors observe those signals and monitor their approach accordingly.

You will know quickly whether this is someone who's available for meeting. The person will either respond openly or shut down the conversation with a curt response. Growling, snarling, and reddening in the face are generally indications that the person is not interested in meeting anyone.

Although turning random connections into productive relationships presupposes an outcome, we have to be respectful toward all those we encounter. Yes, you have a goal, but unlike a heat-seeking missile that finds its target but might destroy everything in its path along the way, you will drive *gently* toward your destination as a successful random connector. We all want to be regarded by others, and no one wants to feel as if he or she is being used only for influence and connections. So although you may have a goal in mind, you want to find your way there gently, preserving the relationship while ultimately discovering opportunity.

Chapter at a Glance

- People in situations designed for networking offer implied agreement to meet.
- People are likely to be more cynical of being approached by a stranger in making random connections than in situations designed for meeting.

- How you approach someone makes all the difference in the response you get.
- Avoid the creep factor—not theirs, yours!
- First assess the other person's level of receptivity based on obvious and subtle clues.
- Don't be afraid to allow a few seconds of silence before and between sentences.

14

Seize the Moment

Based on your assessment of the other person's level of availability combined with your degree of readiness, there is that split second during which you initiate contact. This is that instant when you transition from complete stranger into a potential relationship. It happens when one of you says something to the other. And there is *always* something to say when you want to connect. The key is choosing a phrase or greeting that will engage and resonate with the other person.

Once you are in close enough proximity to someone to talk—and once you have assessed the other person's willingness to converse—what you say will depend on a variety of factors. Sometimes you can use scripted opening lines, statements, or questions that will initiate conversation in just about any venue or situation. For example, I think people have been talking to one another about the weather ever since we have been able to utter the words, "Looks like rain on the way" and "Beautiful day, huh?" Although this is okay for starters, it's rather trite and overused, and it generally doesn't lead to a productive follow-on conversation. Ideally, you will want to capture the freshness of the moment, commenting or remarking on something that is happening around you both (other than the weather). It is a discovery process from that point on, one where you guide the interaction toward finding out about each other and discovering whether there is a basis for further communication.

The key to making opening statements is in saying something appropriate to the moment, something that will connect you with the other person and ideally begin to allow you to assess whether and how this might be someone with whom you could have a mutually productive relationship. Your opening statement could be about the other person's experience in the current circumstance, *your* experience in the current situation, or your shared experience. It can be about a conversation clue you spotted, such as a company logo, a lapel pin, or a binder. You can also ask a question. Drawing attention to the environment (again, this doesn't mean the weather) by making an observation about it is a great way to start a dialogue. If you're standing in a line somewhere waiting to order and you, along with everyone around you, are aware that the service is particularly slow, pointing to the workers and saying something like, "I think if they gave everyone a 50-cent hourly raise we might all be moving along a little faster," would capture a common moment in the environment. It would also establish rapport, because you would be aligning with others' circumstance and state of mind. On the other hand, if you are having a great customer service experience, making an observation about it to the person you want to connect with, something along the lines of "There's a reason this company consistently ranks among the best firms to work for," would more than likely gain agreement and provide a starting point for a conversation. Asking a question is also effective. Both of these break the ice, enabling you to gauge the person's availability for further interaction—and set a direction for the conversation.

It is difficult to proscribe an opening line; the best ones capture something about what is happening in the moment, making them almost impossible to script ahead of time. For example, I met the head of a major human resources consulting firm while on a flight simply by remarking on how adroitly she got in and out of the row we were sitting in when she got up from her seat. She looked like an interesting person, so I wanted to strike up a conversation and find out more about her. I noticed at the same time that, unlike a novice traveler, she got in and out of her seat without pulling herself up with the seatback in front of her. "I can tell you're a veteran traveler," I said. "You must spend a lot of time on airplanes." Surprised by my observation and insight, she smiled and said, "Well, yes, actually I do. How could you tell?" And we were off and running from there. I explained to her how I had made that observation about her, what it suggested to me, how so many novices yank the seatback, and how refreshing it is to be sitting next to a travel pro. In making this observation and sharing it, I (1) initiated contact in a nonthreatening, complimentary way; (2) established my credibility by demonstrating that I was insightful; and (3) was able to transition into learning more about her by asking, "What has you traveling so much, business or pleasure?"

An ideal and appropriate opening statement if you're in a coffee shop is, unsurprisingly, about coffee; how much you like it, what kind you like, tips for making it, how many different kinds there are, a certain specialty beverage that this place makes particularly well, how it makes you feel, how much you drink... the list goes on and on. Just use your caffeinated imagination to fuel the list of remarks you could make.

"I couldn't help but notice..." is a fabulous way to gently insert yourself into what otherwise would be someone else's business. This statement implies that you weren't *intending* to be nosy, but you just couldn't resist noticing/stating/observing—and who could, given the intriguing nature of whatever the other person is saying or doing?

Opening statements or questions needn't be profound or complex. To the contrary, a simple comment or observation creates the common human experience, neutral as it is. Sometimes a highly personal comment proves most effective, because it shows you're willing to reveal something. This in turn gives the other person permission to reveal something as well. It also shows your transparency, which identifies you as safe and credible to the other party.

Every venue offers something to which you can relate or remark upon. I was once on an elevator and shared with the other passenger (in a friendly, wondrous way) that I dream about being on elevators that go sideways. Lo and behold, she said she did, too, and from that moment on we were on our way—in more ways than one. "Do you spend a lot of time on elevators?" I asked, moving toward uncovering what she does for a living. Turns out she manages a team of service technicians, and that conversation led me to the name of the vice president of service for a friend of mine who was in the job market for such a position.

I also recently met a woman on the subway. And by the way, I could have taken a cab that day, but knew I would be more likely to meet people if I put myself in public transportation. She was carrying (dare I say, struggling with) her roller suitcase down a long flight of stairs. She was already toward the bottom by the time I noticed her, so it was too late to offer to help. However, I did manage to make one simple comment that drew the biggest smile I saw all day—and triggered a conversation that went on for the following 20 minutes. I simply said, "They should invent a rolling suitcase for walking down stairs." It was a perfect way to show empathy for her circumstance, and it led into the most natural conversation about how much she travels, why she travels, what she does for work, and what other kind of inventions we could imagine to make travel easier.

I discovered that this woman works for a major fast food franchises opening new stores, hiring key personnel, and designing marketing programs for the launch. What a perfect connection for me. Now I have a friend, a contact, and a potential new client.

Because most of us are interacting with some form of technology while we're traveling (laptop, Bluetooth, BlackBerry, or iPhone), making a statement about whatever tool this is can serve as the perfect conversation opener. For example, you could say something to someone working on the latest iPhone release along the lines of: "That's a nice piece of technology; is it everything I hear it is?" This is a natural and effective opening question to a conversation. And of course, "How do you like your (fill in type of technology)?" is the grand slam of conversation starters. Everyone has an opinion about whatever they're using, whether it's their laptop, smartphone, Bluetooth, tablet, or any other piece of electronic gear. This is an incredibly effective conversation starter for turning random encounters into profitable business relationships because it leads so naturally into a question about what the other person uses it *for*—which, in turn, enables you to uncover what kind of profession the person is in. We'll talk more about that later.

It's important to try to match the other person's verbal and nonverbal behavior. If the person tends to use short sentences, follow suit. If the person is walking slowly, you naturally will have to mirror that pace to carry on a conversation. Most people tend to like those who are similar. Ask more questions than you make statements. And try to listen more than you talk.

Show sensitivity to and awareness of the other person as much as possible. Any positive comment you can make about the other person allows you to accomplish this. You can never go wrong with a compliment: nice suit, nice shoes, nice tie, nice purse, nice ring, nice briefcase, and so on. These will get you going in a great conversation direction.

CASE STUDY: Tory K. overheard a conversation and walked into his biggest sale of the year.

As a director of business development in Latin America for a major shoe company that was based in Tennessee, Tory is truly on trains, planes, and buses *all* the time. This provides him with plenty of opportunities to make random encounters and

(continued)

turn them into profitable connections. He did it a few years ago and ended up with a six-figure deal and a long-standing customer relationship.

As Tory tells it:

> I got on a hotel shuttle bus and sat down in front of two guys who were talking about the South Beach Diet and how they didn't think there were enough good recipes. I was in the middle of that diet program and had a few recipe suggestions for them. They had thick Spanish accents, and I had a hunch they were from Puerto Rico—which is part of my sales territory—so naturally, I was especially interested in making the connection.
>
> I turned around and made eye contact with them both, and smiling said, "I am halfway through that program myself, and I know what you mean about good-tasting options; but I have discovered some newer recipes that are actually pretty good." Of course, they both lit up with interest, and we began a great conversation about dieting and food—which allowed me to then ask where they lived.
>
> From there, we were well on our way into a conversation about Puerto Rico . . . and, of course, who they worked for. Turned out they were with a company with whom I had wanted to do business for years. We talked on the shuttle bus, made a plan to get together again later that day, and then had a great meeting that I basically walked out of with an order. Today they are among my biggest customers, and great client friends.

Your opening statement creates the comfort and trust that's so important in a random encounter and sets the stage for further conversation. Table 14.1 lists some possibilities for opening statements to use—and to avoid—based on various venues. Maybe you could think of some of your own for both columns!

Table 14. 1 Conversation Starters: The Good, the Bad, and the Ugly

	Opening Statements or Questions That Lead to Conversation—SAID WITH A SMILE or FRIENDLY GESTURE	Opening Statements or Questions That Make the Person Want to Call Security or Run Screaming From You
Anywhere	How do you like your (laptop, smartphone, tablet, reader, Bluetooth, etc.)? Excuse me, but I couldn't help but overhear you say something about (topic). Is that your line of work? How is your day going?	I hate when I get dressed in the dark and then find out later that my socks don't match. I haven't had a drink in two days, and I'm starting to get the shakes.
Someone in an airport or travel-related venue	Where are you headed? Going out or coming back? Let's hope they serve more than a bag of pretzels. The glamour and romance of air travel is but a distant memory.	Have you been to the new seafood restaurant here in the airport? It's the bomb.
Someone in a clothing store	That's a great outfit. Do you have to dress up for work?	I wouldn't wear that. That's why I have my girlfriend help me pick my outfits.

(continued)

Table 14.1 Continued

	Opening Statements or Questions That Lead to Conversation—SAID WITH A SMILE or FRIENDLY GESTURE	Opening Statements or Questions That Make the Person Want to Call Security or Run Screaming From You
Someone at a wedding	Beautiful setting for a wedding. Are you with the bride or the groom side? I understand they're going to (place) for their honeymoon.	This is her second and his third. You'd think by now they'd give up on it. I think she's pregnant.
Someone in a coffee shop	Thank the gods above for caffeine! Have you ever tried their super bold? It's really good.	Sometimes they'll give you a free refill if you tell them you spilled the first one on your way out the door.
Someone in a copy shop	Are you your own marketing department, like I am? (Remarking on something they're working on) That's really nice looking. Where will you be using that promotional piece? Have you found brochures to be effective in promoting your business?	I usually have my assistant pick up my stuff. Who came up with *that* design?
Someone reading a newspaper	So what's new in the world?	I think they ought to throw all those bums out of office.

Someone carrying a heavy piece of luggage or loaded down with a suitcase, briefcase, laptop case, etc.	That looks like a recipe for a trip to the chiropractor. Wow, you look like you're ready for anything!	Running away from home? You know, I really think most of us have too much stuff! I just don't understand why people have to hold on to everything they've ever owned!! Have you seen the show *Hoarders*?
Someone on an elevator leaving the office well after 5:00	So, was it a good day? (Looking at your watch) Well, I have a feeling the company got their money's worth from you today!	I'm sure you're not getting paid enough to work this late.
Someone reading a book	Good book? What's it about? Nothing like a good book, huh?	That looks like a really dull book. I read that! (and then give away the ending)
Someone wearing a sweater at the very beginning of autumn	Wow, that's the first time I have seen anyone in a sweater this season. I guess there's no denying that cooler temperatures are upon us.	Isn't it a little early for a sweater? What a lousy reminder of what lies ahead.
Someone walking a dog	How cute. What's its name?	Is it a male or female, mind if I take a look? I've heard that breed is really difficult and ends up turning on its master.

A simple yet relevant comment, observation, question, or remark that captures a shared experience or circumstance is sure to trigger a nice connection. Focusing on the other person, and saying something that resonates with him or her, creates a comfortable start for both parties.

Chapter at a Glance

- There is always something to say to broach a conversation with a stranger. However, avoid commenting on the weather.
- Remarks about a common experience or situation are great for building rapport.
- Asking about how the other person likes his or her personal technology is sure to get a meaningful response.
- Compliments are almost guaranteed to start a positive conversation.

15

Get on Their Wavelength

Most public venues carry a veneer of unfamiliarity and personal privacy, sometimes even cynicism. People don't typically appear open or available for friend making or network building in public places. However, it usually doesn't mean they don't want to; it's just that they don't think *you* want to. There is also that creep factor we mentioned earlier—that fear that the person nearby or approaching is a weirdo. That's why the way you initiate conversations and build the rapport is critical to making a successful connection.

People build relationships in real time and over time. From the instant you attempt to break through another person's privacy barrier, either verbally or nonverbally, he or she will have to decide whether or not to engage in conversation with you. Your tone of voice, body posture, eye contact—and yes, that universal gesture of friendliness and approachability, your smile—will all be the key success factors in breaking through the veil of anonymity. The other person will be assessing you as the conversation progresses, checking you out, determining whether you are safe, secure, and, well ... *normal*. A sense of comfort will settle into the conversation over time, and you will be on your way to a new and potentially lucrative association.

The good news is that people like people who are like them. It's just a fact of human nature, and one that's been proven in studies by social scientists. But you needn't be a communication expert to know it's true. Just think about the people *you* are naturally attracted to; chances are, they're a lot like you.

And because people like people who like them, or at least who *are* like them, it's essential to align yourself with your new acquaintances from the start. That means getting on their wavelength, being curious about them, and showing interest in what they're interested in.

Not long ago, I found myself sitting next to someone on a small airplane who was traveling with a cat. I should mention that I don't have a natural affinity for cats; I am a total and lifelong dog person. So even though the furry creature was in a travel cage, it was still a cat—I was going to spend the next 2 hours sitting next to its devoted owner. For me, it was a little too much feline familiarity.

However, veteran random connectors know that aligning with other people is the golden rule of making successful, meaningful contacts, regardless of our own preferences. So for these few hours, I vowed to find ways to embrace and celebrate cats—and those who own them. I had no idea that at the same time, I would meet a global recruiter for one of the largest consulting firms in the world, an individual who would become a friend, colleague, and resource who would enhance my life and my business in ways I could never have imagined. (That was the woman, by the way, not the cat.)

I knew that people like people who are like them, so I was determined to find a way to like my new seatmate, as well as her furry friend. This was not a time for letting my own sentiments get in the way of making a new connection. It was a time to be other-focused, to be interested, curious, and even fascinated by this person, traveling midday on a business route, with cat in tow. And if I was going to find out what her story was, I would have to override my negative thoughts and feelings about cats—not to mention those who travel with them—lest I limit my possibilities by not even broaching a conversation.

"What's her name?" I asked with interest, gesturing to the cat.
"Sadie," the woman answered.

"What a cute name," I replied, causing this new potential contact to instantly warm up to me. After all, I didn't have to love cats
to get on board with those who do. "Cats are amazing," I added.
"They're very loyal, so much fun to play with, and there's nothing
like a cat curled up on your lap."

Even though I didn't necessarily have experience with cats sitting on my lap, I presumed what I said would be true for my new
traveling companion, so it seemed an appropriate comment to make.
It was my attempt at establishing alignment and common ground.

"She seems to be traveling very well . . . Do you travel with
her often?" I asked, building more rapport and (hopefully) creating
a conversation path about why she travels and what type of work
she does.

Information flowed freely from there as we chatted: she was
moving to a new city for an assignment with her company . . .
recruited senior consultants . . . was focused on the fast-growing
Asia/Pacific region . . . was studying to become a personal coach . . .
wanted to do some part-time work for a firm like mine . . . and oh,
by the way, I would come to discover that her husband worked for
a company that was on my target prospect list.

In random connecting, and life in general, we will always
encounter people who are different from us. That's what makes
life interesting. Our ability to abandon our own, sometimes limited, ideas and beliefs in deference to the other person—to find
what is interesting, even fascinating, about that other person and what
is important to *him or her*—is one of the greatest attributes we can
possess. My cat-loving companion prompted me to abandon my
personal feelings about cats and instead open my mind to the fact
that others *do* love cats—for reasons I may not fully understand or
appreciate. As a result of my ability to keep an open mind, I gained
a valued friend and colleague.

Think about people with whom you just seemed to hit it
off, whether you met them at parties, in business settings, through

mutual friends, or in the neighborhood. Chances are, you will realize it's probably because you and they were—and are—similar in some way or ways.

Sometimes that similarity is a physical one: how you walk, talk, sit, or move. Sometimes these compatibilities are obvious, and sometimes we are aware of them unconsciously. But we've all had the experience of just liking someone immediately. Often those are the people who become our friends and closest associates.

Another way you will connect quickly is by identifying a common interest, hobby, or line of work. Maybe you went to the same school, grew up in the same part of the country, like the same sports team, or like to spend your free time engaged in the same activities. It might even be that you and the other party are in the same emotional state at the time. If you are at an airport and strike up a conversation with someone who is aggravated but you're on cloud nine, having just returned home after closing the biggest deal of your life, you probably won't make a great emotional connection. If, on the other hand, you are also perturbed by some recent experience with the airline or airport service provider, you and your new associate will probably hit it off like great old friends. Consider a sporting event where you and the person next to you are rooting for the same team—or opposing ones. When one team scores and one of you is jumping up and down with happiness and enthusiasm while the other is holding his or her head in disappointment, it's not a match of emotional states. When both of you are jumping up and down with joy and excitement at the team scoring, you know you have yourself an instant best friend.

And often that attraction happens—or *doesn't* happen—in an instant. Most people will decide within the first few seconds of a random encounter whether they want to engage in conversation with you. The other party is assessing whether you are safe or a threat, friend or foe, and whether to engage in conversation or shut you out. And that person will base his or her decision on both conscious and unconscious thoughts about you that stem from how you come across. Therefore, the key to connecting with a complete stranger is to get on that person's wavelength, showing that you are aligned—and it's important to do this quickly (see Table 15.1).

Table 15.1 A Sampling of Things to Match About Others to Create Rapport, Comfort, and Trust

Body posture	Sitting or standing straight
	Sitting or standing slumped
Voice speed	Fast
	Slow
Voice style	Deep
	High
	Clipped
	Smooth
Voice volume	Loud
	Soft
Topics	What's happening at the moment
	Sports
	Current events
	Politics
	Hobbies
	Technology
	Line of work
	Family
	Travel destinations
	Early life places or experiences
	Profession or career
Emotional state	Relaxed
	Stressed
	Happy
	Sad
	Bored
Communication style	Creative
	Rigid authoritarian
	Relaxed
	Humorous
	Serious

CASE STUDY: How aligned interests (and staying in touch) formed the basis of a profitable relationship for Melissa G., an interior designer.

As Melissa tells it:

I had signed up for a full-day bus tour of artistic sites such as museums and galleries in the city where I live. This was a treat for myself—something a bit out of the ordinary and something I had wanted to do for a long time.

I am always interested in discovering new people, so on the tour bus, I made a point of sitting next to someone, rather than sitting alone. Starting a conversation with my seatmate was easy, since I assumed we both must share a passion for art. We fell into an easy discussion of museums we had seen, favorite artists, and places we both wished to visit in the future. There was an instant bond between us.

During our conversation, my new friend mentioned that she had just purchased a town house in the area and was wondering how to decorate it. That was an opening to tell her that I was an interior designer. I did not pitch my services to her, but I *did* mention that I publish an Ezine online that explored various interior design topics. I asked if she would like to be on the free subscription list. She did and handed me her business card with all of her contact information.

The tour ended, and we parted ways, vowing to stay in touch. She received my Ezine, automatically, every few weeks, which served as a touch point for me to stay on her radar. After about two years, she came back to me and asked me to undertake a major redecoration of her entire town house. It was a very enjoyable, and lucrative, assignment.

Sometimes something as simple as a newsletter or Ezine is all it takes to maintain contact with a new acquaintance until that person is ready for your services.

Everyone has a unique communication style. You will be able to tap into this style when you carefully hone your random connecting skills—like tuning a radio to a frequency. It's there; you just need to fine-tune the dial. However, even if you can't pick that up, you can always match the more obvious communication signals. This will let the other person know that you are harmless—and in fact, pleasant.

The alignment can be relative to the other person's voice, body posture, interests, mood, experiences, values—and anything else that makes that person unique. How you talk, sit, or stand and what you say and how you say it will all be evaluated consciously and unconsciously by the other person. And he or she will more often than not respond based on how well you match or align on these factors.

Because most people tend to like those who are similar to them in as many ways as possible, pay attention to and respectfully mirror the other person's communication style as much as you can. The other person will view you as being similar, make him or her more comfortable with you—and, in turn, more likely to open up and share information.

Try to find common ground as soon as possible. Of course, you have to first hear the other party's voice pattern in order to match it. So after making an opening statement designed to gauge availability and create comfort, pay attention to how the other person talks—and what that person talks *about*. If he or she talks loudly, then you can talk loudly, too. If the speech pattern is fast, pick up your pace. Gestures beget gestures. If the speech pattern is short and clipped, speak in short, clipped sentences, too. And try to listen more than you talk.

Chapter at a Glance

- People decide within the first few seconds of meeting you whether they feel comfortable with you.

- Everyone has a unique communication style and "wavelength."
- A smile is a universal sign of receptivity and availability.
- People like people whose voices, styles, emotional states, and other traits and behaviors are like theirs.
- Others will respond best to you when you mirror their voice style, body language, interests, and values.

16

The Importance of Authenticity and Curiosity

Curiosity may have killed the cat, but with nine lives they might have caught a lot of mice along the way. Genuine curiosity—that desire to know—is the lifeblood of good relationships. Showing interest in another person—interest that's wrapped in a genuine desire to discover more about him or her, to get to *know* that person—without judgment, is perhaps the single most critical ingredient in successful relationship building, and certainly in random connecting.

Questions are a pivotal part of random connecting. First, the answers your new acquaintances give you provide the information that you need to assess if, and how, they can be of value to you—and you to them. It also allows you to unlock the gate to conversation; questions show that you are interested in the other person, they make the other person feel valued and appreciated, and of course, they give you the insight you need to determine what potential exists through this person.

To be truly curious, you have to get out of your own world and into the other person's. Truly curious people don't spend a lot of time or effort thinking about their own *personal* interests; they focus on what interests others.

It is very difficult for others *not* to feel regarded, recognized, acknowledged, and appreciated when you are attentive toward them. Yet despite this fact, I am constantly struck by the lack of curiosity among people, especially when they first meet. It's almost as if interpersonal curiosity—the desire to learn more about others, to ask meaningful questions in an authentic desire to get to know the other person—has vanished. Where did it go? What caused people to stop wondering about others? How can we expect others to know that we are interested in them if we don't ask questions that allow us to understand and learn more about them?

Most people, unsurprisingly, like to talk about themselves. If they feel you are genuinely interested in them and their "story," they will share it. In fact, it is so unusual to find someone who asks good questions—and does so with genuine curiosity and actually listens to the answers—that you will distinguish yourself immediately simply by exhibiting this quality.

Find something that is special, unusual, and remarkable about your new acquaintances; your interest will be flattering. What line of work are they in? How did they get to where they are today? Who in their life influenced them to head in that direction? What's their favorite part of their job? These are safe, simple questions. They will give you a glimpse into who each person is, at least on the surface, and they create the path for further conversation while giving you the information you need to determine how you might be of value to one another. You are also earning others' respect and gaining deeper insight about them, all while demonstrating your ability to listen, to care, and to be other-centric. Once you build some rapport, you can ask even more meaningful questions, ones that help you figure out their values and interests. What do they care about most? What's most important to them in their lives?

When you find them fascinating—and everyone *is* fascinating in their own way—they will overflow with information. They will want to tell you more. They will feel respected, appreciated, and acknowledged.

Of course, no one wants to feel *interrogated*, so use a slow pace when asking your questions about the other person; don't ask rapid-fire questions. You want to pose questions in a gentle, nonthreatening way—and always with genuine curiosity and interest.

One answer leads naturally to another question. Imagine the person is a fascinating story that is yet to be told—part mystery, part drama, part comedy, part fiction, part reality. If you meet in a travel venue like an airport or train station, asking simple questions such as "Where are you headed today?" is Random Connecting 101. Then you can delve a bit deeper: "Are you traveling for work?" "How did you get into (the particular profession)?" "Was there a specific turning point in your life when you realized this was the profession for you . . . or where you got a big break that created the path for your success?" "What was the secret to your success?" "Who were your role models?" "If you could do anything else, what would it be?" You will learn about your new acquaintance through these questions, all the while cultivating the rapport that is so essential to relationship building.

The more you inquire, the more you'll discover. That discovery will allow you to mine high-quality information—and you never know where that new information will lead. People are walking, talking stories. And everyone is fascinating in their own way. You will find opportunity in their stories; but you'll never know about these opportunities unless you ask.

I once attended a wedding where a bagpiper was playing for the bride and groom as they walked down the aisle. He was dressed in full bagpiper regalia and blew those horns so all the world could hear. I could have watched and listened like everyone else and assumed he was a bit player in an otherwise lavish production. But I was fascinated by him and was determined to know the story behind him and his craft. While everyone else at the wedding was listening to the music and perhaps thinking about what a lovely touch this added to the ceremony, I was considering where and how I would approach him to get the story behind the story. He was accompanied by his wife, and as luck would have it, they both stayed for the reception, giving me my opportunity.

I began to ask him questions: Was this a side business, or his full-time work? Did he always do this, or was it something he'd begun recently? How and where did he learn? How many gigs does he do in a month—and how often did he play at weddings? Is bagpiping increasing in popularity? What does a set of bagpipes like that cost these days?

As it turned out, this was indeed a side business. By day, he sold job candidate testing materials to companies, something closely aligned to my business. We have spoken about how I can integrate his product into my offerings, and I anticipate we'll do business together at some point.

But the big surprise came through his wife. How could I have predicted that she is a professor at the Art Institute of Atlanta? In chatting with her, she asked if I would be willing to be a guest lecturer at an upcoming class. Six weeks later I was standing in front of 20 marketing majors, sharing my insights and learning from them about the issues and challenges facing young job seekers. I found out about a dynamic educational forum. I found out about new directions. I expanded my network, and all from a random encounter at a wedding with a bagpiper.

Things About People to Be Curious Of
- What they do for a living
- How they got into their line of work
- How long they've been in their field
- What they like most about it
- Where they see their industry or business heading
- What they think have been the biggest changes in their industry
- What they would do if they could do anything else

- Where they live, and if they like it
- Where they were raised
- Where they went to college
- Their most influential role models
- The time in their life when they learned the most
- The time of their life they'd go back to if they could
- What they do for recreation
- Whether they have children, and if so, what their children are doing professionally

The art of asking good questions has been lost in our culture, yet almost everyone appreciates when others show an interest in them. Unfortunately, most people seem much more interested in themselves than in others. This is why you distinguish yourself from the crowd when you show genuine curiosity about someone else; you give the person to whom you are talking a chance to feel recognized and valued. At the same time, you gather the information you need to discover what's possible in the relationship.

Chapter at a Glance

- Questions allow you to discover possibilities.
- You distinguish yourself from others when you are truly curious.
- Most people like it when others show interest in them.
- Asking questions prompts you to draw people out and gain deeper insight into who they are.

17

Focus on Your New Connection

Can you think of instances in which you've interacted with a truly great communicator? Do you remember how it felt? Probably like you were the most important person in the world in that moment. That feeling most likely stemmed from the way the other person looked at you—straight in the eyes. Or the way in which the other person listened to you, hearing what you said and understanding the meaning and feelings behind it. Maybe it was how the new connection avoided external distractions and stayed focused on you and only you.

Extraordinary communicators are fully present when they communicate and interact with another person. That's the hallmark—and secret—of great interpersonal communication (see Table 17.1).

If you want to make high-quality connections with complete strangers, you will want to exhibit those same characteristics by focusing on your new acquaintance instead of on yourself. The difference between a random connector who walks away from an encounter with a name, phone number, e-mail address, and agreement to

Table 17.1   How Communication Skills Impact Relationship Quality

When You Are...	You...
Only pretending to be interested in the other person	Lose that person's respect
	Indirectly offend and insult
	Prevent the relationship from developing
	Don't absorb quality information
	Have short conversations
	Don't create a basis for meaningful follow-up
Moderately interested in the other person	Establish a moderate amount of credibility
	Show you care
	Pick up insights about who that person is and what he or she does
	Have average-length conversations
Genuinely interested in the other person	Gain that person's respect and admiration
	Differentiate yourself as a top performer
	Get high-quality information about that person's needs, goals, challenges, hopes, and dreams
	Have conversations that lead to topics beyond the obvious
	Will have a potential new contact who likes you and wants to continue to be involved with you

speak again and someone who walks away empty-handed is that the successful person focuses on the person he or she is connecting with. Success involves being other-centric, that is, making the other person the center of the conversation by letting him or her talk and act as if he or she is the most important person in the world.

An important caveat here: There is a big difference between those who talk about themselves without being asked, as if what they have to say is of interest to everyone else, and those who are asked to talk about themselves to a ready and interested other party.

Learning what others like or don't like, what they care about, what they've done, where they've been, what they think—their stories, personal history, observations, and insights—are all of great interest to someone who is curious.

Since people generally like to talk about themselves, you are most effective when you prompt them to do so, specifically, by asking questions. If you encounter someone randomly and want to talk about yourself, make sure the other party is interested—and that what you have to say is engaging, unique, insightful, captivating, fascinating, and new. Otherwise, do more listening than talking, at least in the beginning.

There's a story about an older gentleman who meets a young woman at the coffee shop he frequents. They end up spending hours together talking, during which she used the vast amount of time asking all kinds of questions about him and the story of his life, his experiences, his career, his interests, and so on. For hours she asked, he answered, and she listened. When he got home late that afternoon, he shared with his wife that he had met this young woman at the coffee shop and they had talked for hours. "What was her name, and what does she do?" the wife asked, showing interest in his afternoon. "I don't know," he said, "but she sure was fascinating!"

Being other-centric isn't just about letting the other person talk; it's about listening and responding to what that person is saying. We know from our own experience what it's like to interact with someone who is merely pretending to be interested in what we have to say, going through all the motions but clearly uninterested. Their eyes wander, their attention drifts, or their responses are unconnected to the conversation (See Table 17.2)

When you want to connect with a complete stranger and create a successful relationship, there is nothing more important in that moment than *that person*. Your ability to listen, focus, track, and respond appropriately will build the credibility and mutual respect that paves the way for a meaningful—and hopefully mutually rewarding—interaction.

Table 17.2   The Differences Between Unfocused and Laser-Focused Communicators

Unfocused Communicators	Semi-Focused Communicators	Laser-Focused Communicators
Have wandering eyes	Look at the other person	Have nothing but the other person on their mind
Make irrelevant responses	Respond appropriately	Make consistent eye contact
Talk about themselves more than the other person	Let the other person know they're listening	Respond with comments that add value to the conversation
Check their smartphones in the middle of conversations	Ask relevant questions	Play back what they heard and check for understanding
Change topics often	Allow the other person to lead the conversation	Ask highly relevant questions that lead to high-quality information
		Make it safe for the other person to share information about himself or herself
		Pick up subtleties about what is being said and "listen" for the meaning behind the words
		Delve below the surface

People appreciate when others listen to them. It garners mutual respect. And it separates you from the pack in random connecting. It enables you to move the conversation and relationship toward productive outcomes, because it tells the other person you care about and respect him or her.

When you are fully and completely focused on other people, you look at them. You track what they're saying. You listen to the words they're saying and the meaning behind those words. You ask for clarification and elaboration. You send verbal and nonverbal signals that let them know you're paying attention and are interested in what's on their mind and in their heart. You may not necessarily agree with everything that they're saying, but you hear it, you acknowledge it, and you respect the person's right to express it.

Good listening is an attribute of effective communicators, with everyone and in every situation. It is especially important in random connections, because you have to overcome the fact that you're a stranger. So your interpersonal skills have added significance. Good listening doesn't only help build your credibility; it gives you the information you need to know what's possible in the relationship. By listening carefully and attentively, you discover not just what your new connection does for a living but who that person is, what he or she needs, and what's important to that person.

Chapter at a Glance

- Great communicators focus solely on the other person.
- When you give the other person your full attention, he or she feels respected and regarded.
- Use your comments and gestures to let the other person know you are focused on him or her.
- Listen more than you talk.

18

Discover the Buried Treasure

How do you know exactly what kind of potential this random encounter represents? Is this person someone who runs a department in a company? An entire company? Is this new connection an investor? A small-business owner? Retired? Undergoing a career transition? Maybe this person is none of the above but well connected to all the right people around town. Knowing what *you* are looking for—having a clear idea of your primary outcome—will allow you to guide the conversation to discover what is possible through your new connection.

Of course, you don't want to come across as someone who's disingenuous or blatantly hunting for leads. However, once you have initiated a conversation and proved you're not going to steal the other person's identity, you will want to determine whether that person is, in fact, someone worth knowing. Sure, everyone has something to offer; it could simply be good company for the ride (or the wait, or the party). And everyone knows someone who's worth knowing. But if your long-term goal is to expand your business by expanding your network, your short-term goal is to determine whether this particular individual's position, personal/ professional network, or knowledge can be useful to you.

Qualifying your new friend and determining whether he or she represents an opportunity for you is an essential step in successful random connecting. Use your goals to determine whether it will be beneficial to pursue the conversation. After gauging the person's willingness to engage, and starting with neutral questions or statements, you want to get to the meat of the matter: What does this person do for a living? Whom can this person connect me to? And is there something here that I can leverage for our mutual benefit?

You'll want to assess quickly whether this individual is someone of influence. If you are selling a product or service, you want to determine whether your new connection is a decision maker with buying authority and money to spend. If you are seeking a job, you will want to assess whether this person has influence over hiring or can introduce you to people who do. You will have a profile— either formally or in your mind—of the type of individual who represents your best potential lead.

Time is your greatest ally, as well as a precious, finite resource, so you want to spend it where it will do you the most good. There's an old story of an elevator salesman who was having a terrible time getting customers. He was sure he was doing everything right and couldn't figure out why he wasn't making sales. "I'm very professional when I talk to my prospects," he said. "I know my products very well, so I think I am very believable when I discuss them. I listen well, and my presentation is very engaging. I just don't know what I'm doing wrong."

He finally gave up trying to figure it out himself and decided to ask his manager to spend a day with him in his territory making sales calls. Wanting to help in any way he could, the manager agreed to go along and see if there was something this eager but desperately unsuccessful elevator salesperson was doing wrong.

It didn't take any longer than their first appointment for the manager to identify the problem. The salesperson was calling on owners of one-story buildings!

The lesson here? Knowing your ideal customer or target contact's profile is crucial in making effective random connections. If the person isn't in your sweet spot, you will be having a completely different conversation than if that person represents the pot o' gold you've been dreaming of.

My best type of random connection target is an executive in a professional services or business-to-business company who uses external resources (read "consultants") to help improve their company's performance, especially revenue growth. So after breaking the ice and establishing some rapport, I guide the conversation toward their line of work—sometimes going there immediately and directly, sometimes a little more slowly, depending on how the other person is responding. If the person is open to conversation, I ask the million-dollar question: "So what line of work are you in?" And I ask it sooner rather than later. If the new connection seems at all reticent, I might build the rapport a little more before focusing on the outcome. But I know what I want to know about the other person, and I try to get there as fast as I can, while always ensuring the person feels validated and respected regardless of his or her leveragability.

I uncovered opportunity quickly on a recent subway ride. A simple comment of mine opened the door to a high-potential conversation with a person who appeared ready to exit the train at the next stop. I noticed that this individual was carrying a backpack featuring a logo from a company I was interested in approaching. After a quick exchange about the fact that the air-conditioning on the train wasn't working very well, I directed the conversation to something more productive. "So do you work for those guys?" I asked, motioning toward the logo.

"Yes," she replied.

"That company is doing some really cool stuff," I said. "What do you do for them?"

She explained that she was in product marketing, which happened to be the target of my inquiry. I asked if she would mind giving me the name of the director of marketing and if I could follow up with her later on. She gladly provided the name and gave me her contact info, along with an invitation to send her an e-mail—all of which occurred between subway stops.

A conversation with a complete stranger is a discovery process, one where you guide the interaction toward finding out about each other and determine whether there is a basis for further interaction. Determining whether the individual is of value to you is an essential step in successful random connections. Of course, everyone has value in *some* way, but some have more than others or are offering exactly what you're seeking. Based on your goals and your ability to determine the other's contact value as quickly as possible, you very well may find yourself uncovering a business or career opportunity beyond what you ever thought possible.

Chapter at a Glance

- Have a clear profile of the kinds of people who are your best potential connections.
- Know what you want to know.
- Assess whether the person you are talking to can be of value to you, while preserving the relationship.

19

Leave No Stone Unturned

Knowing the profile of those you want to meet is essential for maximizing your random connecting efforts. And these people don't always have to be directly involved in buying something from you. Their value may lie in their ability to direct or introduce you to people who can. Maybe they work for a company; maybe they work for themselves. If you are seeking an employment opportunity, they might be directly responsible for hiring; or maybe they are simply influential in the process.

The ability to assess your new connection's precise leverage point requires multiple levels of mental processing. In other words, you have to concentrate on a few things at once. To begin with, you have to broach the conversation in a friendly, nonthreatening way and attempt to build some rapport. From there, you steer the conversation in a direction that will help you gain the information you need to determine where the opportunity exists. If you're in the business world, seeking new customers, a new employer, or new contacts within a target company, you will, of course, want to know this person's line of work.

Asking high-quality questions with a sense of authentic curiosity will help you build an interpersonal connection and assess the opportunity. Once you know where this person works, it's very natural to then ask what exactly that person does for the company. It's an intuitive, logical, sequential conversation path of information gathering that does not threaten or intimidate your new contact. As you gently direct the exchange to uncover this basic information, listen carefully to the answers while focusing on the person and considering how his or her professional affiliation and/or specific job function can be useful to you—and how you can be useful to your new contact.

When you meet someone who you think has value as a contact, think about how to leverage that person during your conversation. Ask yourself how this person could be valuable to you. Is it through direct influence or the ability to introduce you to someone else? Is it from something that you can learn from him or her, an opportunity within this individual's company, or perhaps even a different channel? Also determine where and when the best time is to act on this; is it now, or later, when the person is back in the office on his or her home turf?

It would be wonderful if everyone we met had resources they could control or allocate directly at their immediate disposal. Sometimes they do, and sometimes the way that they can help you exists in their extended sphere of influence. You'll ideally make random connections with people who you can leverage directly—people who will buy something, hire you, or invest in your company. But everyone you meet has an extended sphere of influence, and this is often where the greatest opportunity rests.

Every contact you make has *some* value, and there's something important to keep in mind here: it's not just where this person works now that could help you out, but where this person worked before—and where he or she might end up working in the future. It's not just a person's direct authority to make purchases that matters; it's whom that person can introduce you to. It's not just what a connection does; it's what that person's family and friends do. If you want to expand your business, career, income, and life, then figure out how to make the most of everyone you meet.

Even people who aren't in your target profile can often be conduits to others.

The circle of influence almost everyone has includes:

- Coworkers at their current employers
- Coworkers at their past employers
- Industry colleagues
- Customers
- Vendors
- Spouse
- Children
- Parents
- Extended family members
- Friends
- Neighbors
- Personal service providers, such as attorney, accountant, financial planner
- Networking associates
- Fellow college alumni

I once met a woman at an outdoor café whose son worked for a major company with which I had been trying to do business. After a 15-minute conversation with this stranger, I had gained her son's name and contact information. I was on the phone with him the next day and was able to gain valuable insights about his company's strategy and key decision makers.

Everyone you meet provides some kind of networking opportunity; sometimes it's just in the form of being a conduit to someone else who has the influence, authority, or buying power you *really* want. Creating profitable business relationships through random networking is often a result of the stepping-stones you put in place to get to the person who will do you the most good. It's a process, and even if you determine that the person you are talking with is not a person of influence, there's a good chance that he or she knows

someone who is (see Table 19.1). If you manage your interaction
with the initial person effectively, you can come away with invaluable
networking information—be it names, opportunities, tips, or insights
for how to get to the people with direct influence.

Sometimes people you meet can give insights about those you
want to meet. In cases like that, getting inside information about
them and their degree of influence is a random connection success.
If you are selling to the corporate market, then it's invaluable to discover exactly who's who—and to verify who *really* has the power
to make buying decisions. Titles don't always reflect where the true
buying authority sits within an organization, so your best insights

**Table 19.1 Everybody Has Something to Offer, Even If
It Isn't Obvious**

If the initial random contact is...	He or she may be valuable to you by introducing you to...	
Retired from a company	Key people who are still with the company	**Who, in turn, can possibly buy something or direct you to someone who can help you**
A former employee of a company	Former coworkers who are still with the company	
At a company but in a noninfluential position	Senior executives of the company or department managers	
In a field that's not related to yours	A spouse, parent, child, or sibling	
A stay-at-home parent	A spouse, parent, child, or sibling	

will come from someone on the "inside" who can tell you who really calls the shots.

A few years ago I found myself next to an older gentleman who was traveling from Atlanta to the Northeast. I knew nothing about him except that I wanted to know more. Distinguished looking as he was, I could tell he wasn't in the prime of his career; yet he had the distinct look of success about him.

"Where are you headed?" I asked with simple and sincere curiosity.

"To see my grandchildren in Pennsylvania," he responded.

"How fabulous," I said, thinking to myself, *Likely retired…out of the mainstream…nice man but probably not leverageable.* However, I kept an open mind and decided that I would pursue this random encounter and see where it might lead. "How many grandchildren?" I asked, staying on the level of pure personal relationship building.

"Three," he replied.

As these few moments of preliminary conversation unfolded, I began to get a hunch and continued to guide the conversation in an attempt to find out whether he was in fact retired and what he was retired from. I thought to myself, *Maybe he knows people in his old company, especially if his retirement was fairly recent.* I wanted to open a conversation pathway that would allow me to discover what he does or did and what he is really all about.

"It must be great to have the time to travel like this," I suggested.

"Well, yes, one of the great benefits of retirement," he replied. "I looked forward all my life to having this opportunity with my family."

Wanting to keep the conversation alive and build rapport, I lobbed back, "I look forward to having the same opportunity when I retire, *if* I ever get to retire," I said with a smile. "So how long have you been retired, and from where?" I inquired.

What I heard in the next sentence was a random connector's dream: retired, yes, six months ago as CEO of the largest office products company in the Southeast—and the country. And did he still know people there? You bet! All the ones who matter. As I explained what I do and how I offer some unique services for business-to-business companies, he also became intrigued. He was more than happy to provide names of key execs who would surely take my calls if I just mentioned his name.

This ex-CEO knew everyone. And he was happy to share the information with me. Of course, since he was no longer actively involved in the business, he clearly did not have any direct influence in decision making. But he was a gold mine of information about the people who still did. He told me who ran the marketing organization and the general direction that the marketing strategy was taking (as best he knew)—and he invited me to use his name when approaching those key people.

Within six weeks of this random encounter, I was sitting in a conference room at company headquarters with the three top marketing executives. The CEO's suggestion that I get in touch with them carried enormous weight in getting me on their calendars. I had instant credibility and a receptive team of decision makers who found great value in my presentation—all because I met a grandfather on his way to visit his grandchildren in Pennsylvania.

At the end of the day, everyone you meet has something to offer, even if it isn't always obvious and it doesn't always monetize. This traveling grandfather didn't have to be the retired CEO of a multimillion-dollar company to be worth meeting. Had he been a service technician at the same organization, he would certainly know who ran the department, the division, and maybe even the entire company. And if not, I would have opened a conversation pathway toward his third sphere of influence: family members. I would have inquired: "Do you have children?" and "Did they follow your career in office equipment servicing, too?" If they didn't, I'd ask, "What line of work are they in?" And don't forget spouses: "Does your wife understand technical talk at the dinner table?... Oh, so she is in a different type of work...What does *she* do?"

You can direct the conversation in any way you want, uncovering what you want to know by creating natural conversation pathways, all the while building rapport, processing what you're hearing, and keeping in mind your ultimate goal of finding the best leverage point with your new connection. It may sound like a lot to juggle, but if you keep these points clearly in mind, it gets easier with practice.

Most of the time all you have to do is ask. Simple questions will do the trick: "Do you know the person in your company who is in charge of (whatever your area of interest is)?" Or "Do you know anyone in HR who is responsible for recruiting?" When you are getting acquainted with a random connection who mentions that he or she has grown children, you could ask at the appropriate time, "So what line of work are your children in?" If someone mentions knowing someone who you would like to meet, you can simply ask, "Would you mind giving me an introduction?" You may find your way to an influential person simply by asking about your new connection's sphere of influence.

Exceptional random connectors know how to optimize every contact they make. That's why it's so important to make every connection you can and pursue every one for what it's worth, as well as where it can lead. It's also why it's so crucial to regard every connection you make as worthwhile, valuable, and leverageable.

Chapter at a Glance

- Everyone you meet has something to offer.
- Sometimes the value of your new connection is through whom they know.
- As you build rapport through your conversation, think about how the person can be of value to you.
- Often it is through someone's extended sphere of influence that he or she can help you the most.
- If the person doesn't fit your target profile, ask for introductions to others who may.

20

Be Clear on Your Own Value Proposition

A successful random encounter will benefit both parties. In fact, the more you demonstrate what (and sometimes who) you have to offer, the more likely the other party will want to associate with you. You will often be the one who reaps the most from the connection you make, at least at first. You may come away from the conversation with a name, an insight, a key piece of information, a chance to make a proposal, or even a sale itself. And although it's impossible to predict what you will get from a random conversation, successful random connectors know they have to bring value to the conversation if they are going to create credibility. They also know what that value is (see Table 20.1). They are confident and self-assured about what they know and have to offer. This is why it's essential to be clear in *your own* mind about your value proposition; it will help build your credibility in the eyes of your burgeoning connection.

Table 20.1 Ways to Describe What You Do That Build Credibility, Engage, Compel, and Get the Other Person to Want to Do Business With You

Descriptions That Don't Create Perceived Value	Descriptions That Create High Levels of Perceived Value
I'm a mechanical engineer.	I build systems that result in greater efficiency for manufacturing plants.
I'm a Realtor.	I help people sell their houses quickly, at the highest possible market rate.
I'm an organizational development consultant.	I show companies how to align their people with their processes to create highly productive corporate cultures.
I sell cars.	I help people drive the automobile of their dreams, for less money than they ever thought possible.
I'm an artist.	I bring beauty into people's lives.
I do personal coaching.	I enable people to find more satisfaction and gratification in their personal and professional lives.
I'm a recruiter.	I help companies find and hire the best talent in the market.
I do multilevel marketing.	I help people realize their dreams of managing their own destiny.
I'm a financial planner.	I show people how to create financial security and achieve their goals of financial independence.

CASE STUDY: A random encounter and a confession to a complete stranger while on vacation in Aruba leads to a lucrative opportunity for David A.'s firm.

David runs a successful executive recruiting practice; however, he knows that what he *really* does is help companies grow by attracting the best talent. He struck up a conversation with a complete stranger while on vacation in Aruba—and landed a huge client for his firm. As Dave explains it:

I was in Aruba with my wife, and we passed many daytime hours shopping at the resort stores. One particular store had a seating area set aside for husbands and boyfriends to wait while their female companions browsed the merchandise.

I took a seat and began chatting with the man next to me. We developed an instant rapport when I said shopping for clothes with my wife was not my favorite activity. After a few more exchanges about the obligations we husbands carry, I asked where he was from.

My ears perked up when he mentioned Silicon Valley, as that is where many of my best clients are. After comparing notes on our hometowns, the transition to asking what he did for a living came naturally. Turns out he was the CEO of a midsize software company.

As I asked about his company's services and specialties, my new friend grew increasingly excited as he spoke about some of the innovative products his company was working on. I saw this as a cue to position myself as someone who could add value to his company, so I asked, "Do you intend to continue growing the size of your company?"

He replied with an emphatic, "Yes."

That's when I had my golden opportunity: "I can help you do that," I responded with a big smile. A quick overview of my firm's services followed, along with an exchange of contact information.

I called my new acquaintance when I got back to Philadelphia. He remembered our conversation clearly and put me in touch with his vice president of sales. It was easy for me to win the VP's confidence, since I had been referred by his CEO!

That company became one of my five biggest clients. And it all started because I confessed to the person next to me that I don't really like to shop for women's clothes.

You bring value, either through what you know, what you sell, what you do, or who you know. And understanding the value you offer is essential in creating credibility for yourself and direction for the conversation. As discussed previously, you want to focus on the other person and how that person can be of value to you. However, keep in mind that Favor Avenue is not always a one-way street. At the end of the day, your ability to help *the other person* is what makes the connection work. Besides, it is your offering that will monetize the relationship—and no one will spend money on your product, hire you, invest in your company, or otherwise commit their precious resources to you if they don't perceive that they will get something in return.

My title is sales readiness and messaging consultant. However, that's just a description of what I *do*. It doesn't really reflect the value I bring to companies and individuals. So when I am asked about my profession, I say, "I turn reputations into revenue." This speaks to the outcome I create, and it's the outcome people want. From that point, I can explain how I do this and what that process involves. And when I explain my job this way, people light up. Even if they don't know exactly what it entails, they appreciate that it's clever and results-oriented.

Your value comes in many ways. What you know—your subject matter expertise—can be incredibly useful to others. What you provide through your service can have great value to others. The way you deliver your product or service can represent a profitable return for the other person. Knowing what you know—and knowing how your knowledge, products, and services translate into something of value to others—is the key to effective sales and thus effective random connecting. Getting the other party to place the confidence in you to turn what began as a chance meeting into a business relationship is the golden nugget of turning random encounters into profitable business relationships.

In fact, the higher up the influence ladder you go, the more important your knowledge and expertise will be in establishing your credibility and value to the other person. And while you surely don't want to be a show-off, you *do* want to make it clear to the CEO you just met that you know your stuff. Or make it clear to the director of human resources at a target potential employer that you're at the top of your game. In either case, you want to express the fact that you're the best the marketplace has to offer.

If you are a marketing consultant, you will make a far greater impact by saying you "help companies expand their customer base by identifying and capturing high-profit segments of their market" than by merely saying that you are "a marketing consultant." If you are a supply chain manager, you will garner far more attention from the chief financial officer (CFO) you just met by saying you "enable companies to reduce their costs and maximize profit and quality by creating greater efficiency in their supply chain." And if you're a housepainter, you will be much better off telling others you "improve the visual appeal, maintenance, and market value of people's homes" rather than simply by stating that you "paint houses."

How you describe your value proposition makes all the difference in how others perceive you. Your job title doesn't necessarily adequately describe how you represent value to the other party. Your value proposition comes through when you can explain exactly how what you do makes a difference for the other person or their company. Describing your value proposition in these terms not only will allow you to fully capture others' attention and establish your own credibility faster but will also pique others' interest in what you can do for them—and make them more likely to want to stay in touch.

Chapter at a Glance

- Successful random encounters are mutually beneficial.
- You bring value to others through your product, service, or expertise.
- By describing yourself in terms of the outcome you create, you build credibility and perceived value for yourself in the mind of your new contact.

21

Position Yourself as an Expert

People are valued for their knowledge in today's marketplace. It's not just *who* you know nowadays; it's *what* you know. You have expertise in your field; maybe there's something you know how to do better than anyone else. Maybe you have insights into how others can use what you do to improve their lives. Maybe you have detailed knowledge of industry trends or competitive offerings. Maybe you know marketplace luminaries. Whatever the case may be, there's no better time or place to share some of that knowledge and expertise than when you want to turn a random encounter into a profitable business relationship.

People are looking for solutions to business, career, and even personal challenges. And even if they are surrounded by resources in their day-to-day position, there's always room for a new insight, approach, or observation to help them see things in a new or more productive way. Creativity and innovation are in great demand today, but is in short supply.

As a random connector seeking to enhance other's lives and thereby establish mutually profitable relationships, it all comes down to your credibility and your ability to establish your value by sharing some of what you know. Not *everything* you know, of course—just enough to show that you have expertise. Your new connection will appreciate and recognize that, and he or she will reward that with interest and a desire to engage you as a resource.

Look for opportunities to make value-added remarks as you listen to your new contact; if opportunities don't present themselves, create them. Share what you know—not by acting like a know-it-all, but by presenting yourself as someone who has a command of his or her chosen profession. Let the other party know that you are a pro. An expert. A leader.

If the other person is talking about a specific problem, offer a solution. If the person is talking about a personal goal, offer a way to achieve it. If the person is looking for something, help find it.

Did you just meet a new potential customer? Make a point of understanding what business problems or challenges that person has that your product or service might be able to solve. Have you just encountered someone whose company is building a division and hiring expertise like yours? Position yourself as a top talent whose background is ideally suited for the jobs the company is trying to fill. Does this person have connections in a company or organization you have wanted to access? Let him or her know you have something of potential value for that other company and that you would appreciate an introduction. Is the connection particularly well informed on a topic that can enhance your knowledge and therefore your market value?

Make a point of asking as many questions as you can to learn as much as you can, and then be sure to keep in touch with your new connection as a subject matter expert. Is this new acquaintance someone with whom you have much in common and find you enjoy talking with? Make a plan to get together again, just for the pure enjoyment of socializing.

Adding value to the conversation and demonstrating my subject matter expertise helped me turn one particular random encounter into a highly profitable client relationship. While on a trip to New York, I was sitting in first class next to a man who was engrossed in a Sudoku puzzle book. I had no idea what his line of work was, or for that matter, if he even had a job at all.

Not knowing much about Sudoku—and in the name of authentic curiosity and waiting for the right moment when he put the book down—I asked how long he had been doing these puzzles. He told me that it had been a few years, and I pursued the conversation by asking about the game and how it's played. He explained it was a good distraction from business pressures. Bingo! I found my conversation path: "So what line of work are you in?" I asked. As we began chatting and the conversation unfolded, I discovered that he was the CEO of a large division of a major software company.

As I asked him about his business, his challenges, his goals, and his needs, I kept hearing that they had an issue with customer retention. It was my lucky day; I happen to have a lot of expertise in the subject. So I shared with him throughout the conversation various insights about what constitutes a customer-centric organization, how to build a customer-centric culture, and the internal steps necessary to achieve it. He was obviously impressed and asked for my business card, which I gladly provided. We went our separate ways upon arrival in New York, agreeing to talk again when we both got back home.

As a matter of standard operating procedure, I dropped him a short e-mail that night from my hotel, saying how much I enjoyed meeting and chatting with him and that I would surely follow up per our conversation. My plan was to circle back by the early part of the following week.

Well, as random connection luck would have it, we both ended up on the same return flight the next day…and guess where: sitting next to each other in first class! This connection was meant to be. But had I not sent the note the night before, I would have missed an opportunity to build my credibility and show I was serious about following up. This relationship resulted in a six-figure consulting engagement and an opportunity to build new material for my consulting business.

No one likes a show-off; however, playing small doesn't impress anyone. The key is to walk that fine line between boasting or being showy and demonstrating a confidence and subject matter expertise. After all, if you don't believe in your ability, how can you expect someone else to? Take stock of what you know, think about how your product or service makes a positive difference for others, and don't be afraid to express it.

Chapter at a Glance

- People are seeking new and better ways to achieve their goals.
- Your subject matter knowledge builds your credibility.
- By sharing a little bit of what you know, you will earn the regard of others and position yourself as a desirable resource.

22

If Nothing There, Catch and (Respectfully) Release

As anyone who has ever gone fishing knows, sometimes what you catch is the wrong kind of fish, too small, or otherwise undesirable. In that case, you throw the fish back in the water... hopefully without tearing its mouth out with the hook!

Even though we make a point of exploring every possible way to leverage a new connection, sometimes there's just nothing there—no matter how hard we try to find it. We discussed earlier the importance of knowing the profile of your best prospects and seeking them out, as opposed to those whose role you will not be able to leverage. So what do you do when you apply your brilliant random encounter skills to connect with someone only to determine that person will be of absolutely no benefit to you? Of course you have the choice to continue the conversation if you want to. After all, this might be the beginning of a wonderful friendship—or even your future life partner.

But if you're random connecting for professional or career purposes, and especially if there are other potential contacts nearby who could represent the opportunity for which you've waited a lifetime, you might be best served by bringing the first conversation to a polite conclusion and moving on to the next.

Whatever you'd said up to that point, or whatever your opening question might have been, you can with the same degree of enthusiasm simply let the person know it was a pleasure meeting him or her, that you learned something, and that you wish him or her well. And do it all with a smile and sincerity.

It's like fishing for trout but catching blowfish. You are going to throw the blowfish back into the water, but the blowfish might say, "I know you are fishing for trout, so you have no interest in me, but before you throw me back into the lake, can't you at least tell me you like my gills?"

Chapter at a Glance

- Not every random encounter represents a professional or career opportunity.
- You always have the option of establishing a friendship when there isn't something there to enhance your professional life.
- If there are other connections to be made nearby, refocus your energy there.
- Always be polite and respectful when parting ways.

SECTION
III

Leveraging the Connection

Although random connecting requires that we encounter complete strangers and engage them in meaningful conversation, this process isn't just about meeting people and talking to them. It's about making connections that you can develop into mutually rewarding relationships.

Sometimes that reward comes in the form of money. Sometimes in the form of access to someone or something. Sometimes it's in information we glean from our new association. And sometimes it's all of those.

Many people strike up conversations with strangers. In fact, from my observation it's happening all across the world, all day, every day. And those random meetings likely entail some very interesting discussions. But what has the potential to become a highly profitable connection is all too often left at merely a random exchange. What happens next is up to you.

23

Map the Road to Opportunity

A quick conversation, a fun exchange, or a single shared moment. How many times have you met someone, either while traveling, at a party, at a bar, or in the coffee shop, and left it at simply what it was: a pleasant, perhaps even interesting, one-time conversation?

Now imagine the possibilities that might have materialized had you explored a little deeper, discovered a basis for staying in touch, and followed up with a communication that kept the relationship going and the opportunity alive. Those random connections may very well have changed your life in some significant way.

Bottom line, random connecting is about turning your new relationship into opportunity—something productive for both you *and* your new association. It's of course completely fine to just make friends, and everyone you meet doubtlessly has some value to you and you to them. However, turning random encounters into profitable business relationships is the goal—and that means an out come, a purpose, and an intention.

The difference between someone who likes to meet people and someone who turns random meetings into relationships that materialize into something of great consequence—a bigger bank account, access to people of influence, new insights or knowledge—is that successful random connectors invest the time and effort to follow up, stay in touch, and cultivate the relationship. It's the difference between collecting business cards and gathering business *connections*.

This person might buy something from you, or he or she may lead you to someone who can. At the very least, this new connection could open your mind to something new and worthwhile that will ultimately add to your life or your net worth. But you can't walk into a bank and explain to the teller that you want to deposit the conversation you had with a stranger, nor can you pay your bills with a conversation, even though it might be leading you in that direction. Random connecting has the ultimate goal of turning the new relationship into an outcome, ideally, a tangible one.

As you will see in the following case study of a random encounter, the willingness to invest effort and energy in the follow-up resulted in a desired outcome of benefit and value to both parties.

CASE STUDY: Staying in touch and cultivating a random connection led to a huge career and life-changing opportunity for a recent college grad.

Stephen B. was 23 years old and a recent college graduate when a random encounter on a flight from New York—and some very skillful follow-up—set him on a lucrative and unanticipated career path. As Stephen tells it:

> I was flying home and found myself seated in the last row of the flight. The woman next to me was a standby passenger and had rushed onto the plane just before they shut the doors. I could tell she was a businessperson by the way she was dressed and the fact that she carried a briefcase;

since I was in "career mode," she immediately caught my interest.

Shortly after takeoff, she began flipping through magazine after magazine and tearing out items of interest. I happened to be reading GQ. We started talking about what we enjoyed about our respective magazines and what I thought about men's fashion. Then the conversation turned to what we each did for a living, and I discovered that she was in the commercial real estate industry, specializing in high-end fashion retailers.

I became more and more intrigued as I asked about her business and began to be able to truly see myself in that industry. I finally worked up the courage to ask for her business card. The plane was landing by this time; I was going to be getting off, while she was continuing on. I said that I would be interested in coming to see her to learn more about her business, and she seemed receptive to that suggestion.

We traded e-mails over the busy holiday period. I initially got in touch with her to tell her how much I enjoyed our conversation and referred to something she had said about the challenges of fitting the right retailer to the right location. I made a suggestion about it that she must have liked, because she replied in a positive way. We continued to exchange e-mails and one voice mail about the possibility of a trip to her company headquarters. I researched her company and the commercial real estate industry as a whole in between our exchanges. I became increasingly interested, thinking this might be a great way to combine my passion for sales and fashion.

About a month after that first meeting on the plane, I drove to Birmingham to meet this woman and members of her team on a purely exploratory visit. As it turned out, this meeting led to a job offer, which I decided to take.

(continued)

It worked out fabulously; I got transferred all around the country, helping to manage various projects for the company. One of those trips even led me to reconnect with an old girlfriend who ended up becoming my wife.

I stayed with the firm for five years. If I hadn't met this woman on the plane, and followed up with e-mails and a visit to her company headquarters, I would not have found both the career—and woman—that I love so much and that changed my life forever.

Based on your intended goal—to sell your company's products, your professional services, yourself into a new job, or some such profitable endeavor—you will at some point need to determine whether, in fact, there is a pot o' gold at the end of that road, or at least if there is a good chance of it. This might happen weeks or even months (for big deals, maybe even years) after the first encounter. But it's why you're in it, and you want to leverage your random encounter into a profitable relationship as quickly as you can.

Not every encounter will materialize into a profitable or productive relationship. But if you don't keep an outcome in mind during your conversation, and don't put in the effort to follow up, you surely won't monetize or optimize the potential of your new association.

Depending on how rapidly the conversation progresses, you might even be able to identify the opportunity during that first encounter (as Stephen did). In other cases—and so as not to seem *overly* ambitious (imagine that!)—you might soft sell in the conversation and save your business proposal for a second or third interaction. Rather than immediately addressing your offerings, you can keep the conversation on the level of an interpersonal relationship in this case, holding back on your value statements and instead just getting to know each other. But in any case, effective follow-up can transform a pleasant exchange into a profitable encounter.

Chapter at a Glance

- Pleasant conversations with strangers don't typically change lives.
- The goal of a random connector is to monetize or optimize the connection.
- The ultimate value of a random encounter is directly related to how well you follow up.
- Some connections manifest quickly; others take a longer time.

24

Build Your Momentum and Credibility With a Follow-up

Staying on your new acquaintance's radar is the priority after a first encounter, because time is never on your side. If there is something you want the other party to do—give you the name of someone influential, send you a key piece of information that you referenced during your initial encounter, or, most significantly, meet or talk with you again—you must remain fresh on that person's mind. Even in the best of random encounters—those that involve a fun, exciting, interesting exchange that's full of promise and potential—the impact *will* fade over time if you do not keep it alive. In addition, the anonymity that's inherent in random interactions creates enthusiasm that is situational—and that can therefore dissipate rapidly if you don't act right away. And the importance of following up quickly connects directly to the degree of prominence and influence the other person has. Senior executives have short access windows. As you go down the food chain or toward less influential people or lower yield opportunities, following up is still necessary but relatively less time critical.

Successful random connectors move rapidly to get back in touch with the new acquaintance; they're aware that to wait is to allow them to either forget the encounter or to dismiss the interaction as fleeting and inconsequential. There's also the question of credibility issue at play, as the other party may frequently wonder: *Is this person legitimate or a flake? Was this person just caught up in the excitement of a random encounter, or does this person have something worthwhile to offer? Is this person who he or she says? If it takes this person this long to circle back with me, how important could our conversation really be to him or her?* You don't want your new association wondering about the legitimacy of your initial encounter and taking too much time to contact them allows those questions to trickle into their mind. The Latin phrase *tempus fugit*, which mean "time flies," surely applies here—and it never works in favor of the random connector.

The good news is that following up and staying in touch has never been easier than it is today. You can send a short e-mail saying hello again and referencing the initial conversation or leave a voice mail with a similar message within hours or days after the first meeting. Approaching the situation in this way avoids putting your new connection on the spot, and these approaches are not overly ambitious. They simply are the difference between meeting someone standing in line at the supermarket but never getting a name and meeting someone at the supermarket who owns a company, getting contact info, and sending a follow-up e-mail that leads to a meeting with you the following week. Scenario 1 won't mean much; scenario 2 could change your life.

There are questions or statements you can make at the end of a first encounter that will set the stage for following up and allow you to keep the connection going. Examples include:

- Can we exchange cards?
- What's your e-mail address?

- May I give you a call when you're back in your office and talk with you more?
- When is a good time to circle back with you?
- Are you available to get together for lunch in the next few weeks?
- Would it be all right if I send you an invitation to connect on LinkedIn?
- Can you give me the name and contact info (phone number, e-mail, etc.) of that person you mentioned, and is it all right if I use your name when I contact him (or her)? Or better yet: Can you give me an introduction?
- Would you be willing to take a look at a proposal for (whatever you were talking about)?
- Can I send you my resume?
- Can we get together again? When?

Depending on what you and your new connection discuss and agree to in your initial conversation, you will want to follow up appropriately. Sometimes it's just to build the relationship and keep the communication alive; sometimes your goal is to advance the content of the conversation. Following up could be sending a short e-mail saying that you enjoyed meeting the person, or it might be sending correspondence with some information relevant to what you discussed, such as a link to a website or article. It could even be sending a more complete recap of your discussion that's designed to set the stage for further contact and interaction focused on a specific outcome. Voice mail is also a great way to further personalize the follow-up, since your voice and personality can come through. In all cases, conform your follow-up to make it relevant to the conversation and designed to keep the opportunity alive.

Table 24.1 lists some things you can reference or say in your follow-up to the initial encounter that enable you to optimize and monetize your new connection.

Table 24.1 Match your follow-up to the person's initial level of interest

If the conversation was...	Your follow-up should be...
Unstructured without a specific focus or direction	Designed to build the relationship and provide the basis for staying in touch, with no particular outcome in mind other than that. Examples include simple phrases such as "Nice meeting you and enjoyed our conversation" and "It was great fun talking with you, and I look forward to more enjoyable conversations in the future."
Focused and had a specific direction but didn't end with a clear next step	Designed to build the relationship, cultivate the opportunity, and suggest a next step that will move you toward an outcome. After a sentence or two of polite reference to the meeting (see above), you would direct your comments toward the productive outcome by starting with a comment such as, "In our conversation we talked about (reference his or her areas of need) and how I might be able to assist. I am wondering if we could talk again, either via phone or in person, and explore the possibilities in more detail." Or you could start with, "When we met, you shared some interesting thoughts about your goal to (reference specific goal). I thought you would enjoy the attached article about that very subject. Let me know what you think, and let me know if we can get together again to discuss it in more detail."

If the conversation was...	Your follow-up should be...
Very focused with a specific direction and a clearly understood next step	Designed to keep the momentum moving toward that next step, while reinforcing your role and ability to deliver value. After a sentence or two of polite reference to the meeting (see first box above), you want to restate the key parts of his or her comments, explain specifically how you will make a difference, and then confirm the next step as you discussed it during your initial encounter. You want to use comments such as, "The position you are seeking to fill in your department will be critical in helping the company achieve its long-term growth goals. My experience and skills will enable me to hit the ground running and make an immediate impact. I will call you next Wednesday as agreed and will have the information you requested ready for you at that time."

The journey from initial encounter to monetized relationship requires that you focus, expend energy and time, and always have an outcome in mind. If there's something you want at the end of that road, it's your job to map the territory, check the route, and get there as quickly as possible.

Sometimes you will have made a friend from your initial encounter, in which case a cordial follow-up with will be highly appropriate. But if you've encountered an opportunity that can manifest in something of specific and measurable worth, you will want to keep the focus on whatever the goal is: a job interview, a chance to give an estimate on providing your services, an actual assignment, a sale, access to a third party who is of interest and value to you, or whatever the opportunity may be.

We all want friends, of course, and we all want to meet interesting people. But the ultimate purpose of a random connection is to monetize the encounter in some way. You deliver value in some way; your new association rewards you in return. Your ability to cultivate your new relationship will be the difference between expanding your business, your career, your checking account, and your life or just making a friend.

Chapter at a Glance

- Following up quickly allows you to stay on your new contact's mind.
- The more influential the person you've met is, the more likely that person is to forget you and move on.
- The availability of e-mail and voice mail make following up easier than ever.
- You want to match the content and tone of your follow-up to the initial conversation.
- Keep your goal in mind as you develop and implement your follow-up.

From Unplanned Meeting to Monetized Connection: A Case Study

Everyday encounters in the places to which you journey in your ordinary life can lead to extraordinary opportunities if you are aware, awake, and alive to their possibilities. However, that gets you only halfway there. As we discussed earlier, you can't put a conversation with a prospective client in the bank; you will have to get in touch—and do so quickly—in order to turn the other person's interest into an invoice. You won't increase your salary or job title from merely talking to a potential employer; you will have to circle back with that connection to turn the opportunity into an offer. You simply won't fully know what's possible if there is no subsequent contact.

One of the most fruitful random encounters I ever experienced required a carefully orchestrated follow-up. The meeting involved the president of a large industry association whom I met while traveling to Chicago. It was a midday flight, and he was my seatmate. He was dressed casually with his shoes off, reading a book and nestled comfortably in his seat. This was the level of accessibility I would never have had if I met him at a networking event—or worse yet, in his office. He probably would have had his guard up if we had met at an industry function, fully aware that he was the bull's-eye in the target of a roomful of hungry networkers. The environment would have been hectic, wrought with distractions as countless people engaged in lots of short, superficial, and unmemorable conversations. I might have even been one of them, blending into a sea of faces, elevator pitches, and business cards. This is the environment for high-impact conversations.

But here at 37,000 feet, seat reclined, blanket over the lap, cocktail by his side, and favorite book in hand, we might as well have been sitting in his living room—comfortable, relaxed, and available, the ideal circumstances for quality, engaging, and memorable conversation. Of course, that only created the opportunity; it was up to me to monetize it.

A random everyday connection that doesn't go beyond the initial conversation is nothing more than a friendly chat. You aren't likely to expand your client list, advance your career, deepen your contact base, enhance your subject matter expertise, or grow your bank account with conversations that don't have a follow-on activity. That's why your ability to leverage the connection becomes so essential.

My new industry association president friend provided a perceived purposeful outcome down the line, one that gave me a reason to continue the relationship. He was looking for something, and I could provide it. I had subject matter expertise, and he had a need to share that expertise with his members.

However, this individual might not have been willing to tip his hand and share who he was and what he did with me if I hadn't made a good impression right off the bat. The impact you make during your initial interaction is a critical part of your ability to turn your random encounter into a productive relationship. That's because the other person is far more likely to be receptive and available to you later on if they remember you in a positive way from the beginning. The person you want to leverage is presumably someone of influence, and influential people are far more likely to respond to those who are impressive and memorable. Are you believable? Are you likable? Do you make a lasting impression? This initial encounter is where you establish yourself as legitimate, authentic, and the real deal. And you show the other person that you are someone with something worthwhile to offer.

The formula is simple: ask relevant questions, make appropriate comments and insightful observations, and engage in focused listening to form the foundation you need to cultivate a productive, enduring relationship later on—a win-win relationship of respect, trust, and likability that you can leverage into a mutually productive outcome.

Chapter at a Glance

- The initial encounter is only a starting point; the follow-up is what leads to the payoff.
- A good first impression increases the chances that your follow-up will get results.

26

Create a Basis
for Continued Contact

Making a new connection based on a feeling of mutual respect is essential to leveraging the relationship later on. As we discussed earlier, people like people who like them—or at least those who *are* like them. Therefore, it's essential to align yourself with your new associate from the get-go. That means getting on that person's wavelength, being curious about that person, and showing interest in what he or she is interested in.

To return to the story of my encounter with the association president: I, of course, asked if the book he was reading when we met on that flight was for business or pleasure. "Pleasure," he replied. So I asked what it was about and remarked that I felt reading is a great way to relax. He agreed, with enthusiasm, and went on to tell me about how much he was enjoying the book. It was a spiritual book, something you don't typically find in business settings and something that served as a rapport clue for me. He was revealing something about himself: that he had a spiritual side. Presumably, he was a person with ethics and integrity, motivated to live up to a high standard, and interested in improving himself. It would be easy for me to build rapport with him, because I also have a spiritual side, value self-improvement, and appreciate people who bring ethics and integrity to the business world.

"It would be a great day for corporate America if more people read books like that," I remarked, hoping to establish a bond with him. I went on to ask, "What are the main themes in the book that can be applied to day-to-day life?" I felt that his answers would provide me with a quick and deep insight into his beliefs and value system—among the most powerful levels on which to build a connection—and would therefore make it easy for me to align with and relate to him.

Using trust, credibility, authenticity, and likability as a foundation, you can cultivate the relationship with confidence. But as you learned earlier in this book, you can't fully leverage the connection unless you know what you want from it. You must have a goal in mind, and you can discern this by asking yourself, *What opportunity does this new connection represent?* Is it the person's ability to buy from you? Can this connection's position in his or her company grant you access to others? Does this person have the potential to hire you? Does this contact represent a gateway to new information or resources that will enhance *your* subject matter expertise?

Having a clear understanding of what outcome you're hoping to achieve by making a particular connection provides focus and direction to the conversation. Without this, you don't have a destination and won't know where to steer the conversation. But with the right guidance and a clear intention in your mind, you can learn all the key things about your new connection. You will be finding out about your new connection as you converse, gathering information about where this person works, what he or she does, who he or she knows, where this person lives, what his or her hobbies and interests are, and anything else that will allow you to assess the possibilities for further contact—including, of course, how this person can be of value to you, and you to him or her. This is how you discover the leverage point—the sweet spot where the two of you connect to mutual profit. And when you find it, you will guide the conversation toward it—*delicately*.

I asked high-quality questions when I met the industry association president. I made a point of understanding what the association's issues and challenges were and determining how he was dealing with them. But I didn't do this until after I had built a rapport and established a level of comfort and trust. I discovered as the conversation unfolded that his company had communication problems; the industry was under increasing pressure from the public, and the association wanted its members to be ambassadors for the profession.

I began to formulate a plan in my mind as to how I could help as my new connection was giving me this information. When he mentioned that he was planning an annual conference, I envisioned myself standing in front of their members—lots of them!—while sharing the finer points of effective communication. This was my sweet spot, and in this case, my leverage point. The more he talked, the more I knew that my expertise in communication would be useful to his organization's members as they attempted to speak on behalf of their industry. And at that point I honed in on my goal: to position myself as a potential keynote presenter at their conference.

Chapter at a Glance

- When people like you, they are more likely to pay attention to and respond to your efforts at following up.
- The more you glean about your new connection, the more you can appeal to that person and his or her personality when you follow up or reconnect.
- Identifying what you want from the relationship helps bring focus to your message when you circle back.

27

Add Velocity to the Relationship

Once you have the rapport in place and a basis for further contact, it is up to you to keep the exchange alive. Influential people have busy lives, and the random encounter they've had with you may or may not stay on their minds as much as it does on yours—or as much as you would want it to. Just as massage therapists will never take their hands off their client for fear of breaking the therapeutic connection, successful random connectors will keep new relationships alive through sustained communication. It's your job to turn your random encounter into an opportunity—and that means constantly moving the relationship, conversation, and opportunity forward.

Sometimes you part ways and make a vague agreement to be in touch again. In this case, it's your job to stay on the other person's radar screen as he or she returns to a fast-paced workweek. On the other hand, if you get your new contact to commit to staying in touch by agreeing to some kind of next step upon parting ways, you increase your chances of having a successful follow-up.

A lot of people talk a good game in the moment but flake out in the follow-up. It's rare that someone actually circles back and stays in touch. So that's how to differentiate yourself and build credibility; be the kind of person influential people want to know and with whom they want to be involved.

If there's a specific action step, of course you will respond accordingly. If there is no agreed-upon follow-up, you can stay in touch with occasional notes, interesting links and articles, and other meaningful communication. You can simply exchange e-mails and phone conversations to maintain the relationship.

As I mentioned in the prior chapter, timing is of the essence in following up with a new random connection; you want to keep the relationship alive and leverage the opportunity. Send an e-mail within a day or two of your initial meeting telling your new friend that you enjoyed the meeting, found the conversation interesting, and learned a lot. (Or if you're really motivated, send this message via snail mail on paper. Yes, real paper; it gets attention!) If you have a previously agreed-to action item, reference it and elaborate accordingly. Suggest yet another step.

After landing at O'Hare Airport on that flight, my new association president friend and I walked toward baggage claim. We talked about how and when I should be back in touch with him. "So what's your schedule in the next week or two?" I asked. "Will you be around?" Wanting to increase the chances of a reply based on his preferred method of communication, I asked, "Should I drop you an e-mail or give you a call?"

He explained to me, "I'll be at an offsite meeting for the next two days but back in my office after that. Send me an e-mail toward the end of the week and make sure you give me a link to your website. I have a meeting with the association board in two weeks and we'll be discussing the speaker for the conference, so the timing is good. We can talk on the phone after that."

"You got it," I said. "I'll be in touch accordingly."

In this case, I immediately discovered how this new connection and I could be of service to each other, but sometimes the initial interaction doesn't lead to a clearly defined leverage point or follow-up plan. You may discover multiple areas of leverage, or there might be none that surface initially. It might seem pushy to nail down a specific leverage point in the first interaction in some cases; in fact, sometimes the relationship will be better if it develops slowly. But whether or not you have a defined next step, it's essential to follow up within a few days, lest the memory of your random encounter fade in the mind of your new connection.

Wait a day or two for a reply after you follow up. If you receive the kind of response you want, you are on your way to leveraging the relationship. If your e-mail or voice mail box is empty, simply make another attempt, perhaps asking if he or she received your first one. Inquire if there is anything else you can provide. If there's still no reply, a phone call might be in order, simply to determine whether there is, in fact, something there to pursue.

Sometimes what you thought was interest by the other party might have just been empty encouragement.

However, it's also possible that the new connection is just busy and focused elsewhere for the time being. It's easy to assume lack of interest, believing that otherwise the person would have responded. But successful random connectors never make assumptions about the lack of a reply; they gather the facts before drawing conclusions.

Generally, people don't reply because of one of two primary reasons: they're temporarily too busy, in which case it's just a timing issue, or they're not interested. As a random connector who is following up, you will either reference the topic or action step from the initial encounter or keep the connection going by sending short e-mails focused on the relationship (for example, by asking, "How are you?" and "How are things?"). You can also send along articles, links, or other pieces of information to show you are thinking of the person and to add some value into the relationship. Here are some e-mail examples I've used that you can work with:

Example 1: To the industry association president, where we had a focused conversation and agreed-upon plan for follow-up

Subject line: Our meeting and possible next steps re: communication skills for your members

Hi Pat, I trust this finds you well and that you arrived safely at your final destination in Chicago. I also hope you found the last part of the book as interesting as the first. *(This would remind him of our initial conversation, a part of the discussion that built a lot of rapport between us.)*

(Wanting to keep that level of rapport and bring his attention to the possible business we could do together, I went on to say in the e-mail:) It was a pleasure meeting you and learning about the association and its goals for next year. We discussed how my expertise in effective communication would make an ideal presentation at the conference— providing an entertaining and educational experience for all.

If you haven't already, please take a look at my website (www .topus.com) and then let me know how you'd like to proceed. *(Putting this in the e-mail and getting him to my website would help ensure he continued to have a good impression of me.)* I'd be happy to send you an outline of the presentation, or at least share some thoughts on what it could cover. *(This gives him something specific to respond to.)*

Again, I enjoyed the initial conversation and looking forward to our next one. *(Keeping the door wide open for continued communication.)*

Example 2: Follow up when someone offers to put you in touch with an influential contact

Subject line: Our conversation on shuttle and your offer for key contacts

Hi Tom. I trust this finds you well, and that you remember me from our brief "random encounter" on the car rental shuttle the other day. I hope they were able to get you the vehicle you wanted without too much trouble, and that you were able to find your way to New Jersey without too much traffic! *(This comment would show that I was interested in him and that I remembered what we talked about in our initial conversation, keeping the follow-up very personal.)*

(Wanting to get a specific response that would be of value to me and also reiterate how I might be able to provide value there, I said:) You were kind to offer to give me the names of the key decision makers in the residential lighting group, and I'd like to take you up on it. Can we talk later this week, or is there a better time for me to call you? I believe my program would fit well there, and it would help a lot if I knew the key players in that division. Thanks in advance for whatever you can do on this. Looking forward to your reply and with best regards in the meantime.

Example 3: When there is no specific "business" to be done or follow up on but you want to cultivate the relationship

Subject line: The people you meet in coffee shops and the essence of great leadership.

Hi Karen. I trust this finds you well. When we met the other day at Starbucks we were talking about the traits of great company leaders. Here is an article that you might find interesting . . . it was written by one of the top "leadership gurus" and has some great pointers for anyone who finds themselves in the executive "C-suite." Note the last section about fearlessness as a key trait these days! *(This kind of reference to our initial conversation and the allusion to the article would position me as a professional—someone who is aware of current market trends and who can also be of service by bringing her attention to the article.)*

I enjoyed our conversation and look forward to staying in touch. Maybe we can do lunch the week after next; let me know your schedule.

Best regards until then.

These examples show the great advantage to one-way communication, as it might be much too soon to attempt a two-way real-time follow-up conversation with your new contact at this point. You probably hold "new acquaintance" status in this influential person's mind—and a telephone call might put him or her on the spot. This kind of correspondence allows you to continue to establish your credibility and earn your way into this person's trusted circle before asking for too much too soon.

A short e-mail or voice mail is perfect for nurturing the interpersonal relationship, restating the leverage point from the initial conversation, and/or simply demonstrating your interest and credibility. For example, I sent an e-mail telling the association president how much I enjoyed our "random encounter" on the flight, made reference to the book he was reading and how much I enjoyed hearing about it, and then restated his issues with the association and how I could be a valuable resource. And, of course, I included the link to my website.

Chapter at a Glance

- Follow up within a day or two via e-mail or voice mail, unless a time is already set to call or meet again.
- Reference the meeting in the subject line, comment that you enjoyed the conversation, and recap whatever topic or idea was discussed in the initial encounter.
- Ask for what you want—be it a follow-up meeting, a chance to make a proposal, the names of key contacts, or information per whatever you discussed in the initial conversation.
- If a response comes, reply accordingly and keep things moving forward.
- If you don't receive a reply after two days, send another e-mail asking if the first one was received and if he or she needs anything else from you.
- If there's still no reply, call to assess the situation.

28

Success—Desired Leverage Achieved!

Once you've made a favorable first impression and followed up with some kind of communication, you are moving the relationship toward full leverage. You have established your credibility, uncovered a basis for further conversation, and demonstrated that you are interested in further contact. Now it's time to consummate the opportunity, materialize the leverage point, and monetize the relationship. This is where you materialize the connection. It's where you "close the deal."

You can proceed accordingly based on your new connection's response. If you want the name of a contact in his or her company, now is the time to ask for it. If you're seeking a chance to make a presentation or submit a proposal, now's the time to arrange it. If you want to land a job interview, now's the time to request it. Whatever your goal and desired outcome for the connection, now is your time to go for it.

When I called my association president friend to follow up after his board meeting, we of course started with pleasantries: How are things? How have you been? What's new? From there I asked how the meeting went, whether he was able to present me as a possible speaker, and what the next steps should be.

"You're 75 percent in," he assured me. "They like your topic. Now I need an outline of your talk, a fee proposal, and a more complete bio." Needless to say, I responded right away with the information he requested. From that point, we exchanged a series of phone conversations and e-mails, including some with the association staff, where we nailed down details of the event and my presentation. Three months later, I was standing in front of 150 association members sharing best practices for successful communication—and meeting the president of the national association, a connection that would doubtlessly lead to countless additional opportunities.

Chapter at a Glance

- Once the relationship is in place and a basis for working together has been identified, you are ready to "close" the opportunity.
- Focus your follow-up on the specific opportunity at hand.
- Give your new contact the information he or she wants and "ask for the order."

29

Be Google-ready

Timely and relevant follow-up to a random encounter will keep the momentum moving in the right direction and position you for a successful outcome. However, there's more to the story. With the eye-popping, head-spinning growth of the Internet and its pivotal role as a repository of information about people's personal and professional lives, managing one's online presence has become an essential part of how we present ourselves to the world—and how others perceive us. The likelihood that the people you meet will check you out on the web is growing every day, especially if they have an initial interest in buying from, hiring, partnering with, investing in, or continuing to be involved with you for any other reason.

Your initial random encounter will allow you to establish your credibility, build the connection, pique interest in what you have to offer, and establish a basis for further contact. But even the best in-person random encounter can be undermined by a poor show-ing in a Google search once your new contact accesses the Internet after your meeting. There are countless reasons to manage your web personality, or what I call your "webonality," and establishing

149

legitimacy for yourself and whatever you represented in your initial encounter is at the top of the list. For better or worse, who you are online is who you are in life. And it is increasingly the case these days that if you don't exist online, you simply *don't exist*. To a large degree, a favorable online presence is a prerequisite for professional success. And it's certainly true when used as a vetting tool for those you encounter randomly.

First and foremost, you want to be present online as someone whom others perceive as active and viable in the marketplace. If you don't show up at all, or only minimally, your new contact is very likely to question whether you are for real. Fortunately, it's easy to create a web presence by completing Google, LinkedIn, and Facebook profiles. These three main tools will give you basic online visibility and let you establish the fact that you actually *do* exist. And since you can control the information, you present yourself exactly as you want to.

You should ideally use the Internet to build and enhance your professional identity or brand. When taken to the next level, your online presence will go beyond these three basic profiles to exhibit your expertise, subject matter knowledge, achievements, accolades, and professional reputation.

For example, let's say you are a salesperson for a particular company. A Google search of your name should display your product or service knowledge and recognize you for your industry or customer experience. If you are an independent consultant, you can elevate your status in your potential client's eyes if a search of your name shows your subject matter expertise through links to articles in which you've been referenced, white papers you have written, or marketplace activity in which you were involved. The same would be true if you are in job transition; you will raise your value as a potential employee if online search results of your name differentiate you and convey your value proposition and unique attributes as a candidate.

Table 29.1 lists some key pieces of information and considerations for your online profiles that will help ensure a favorable

Table 29.1 Building a Favorable Online Profile

Type of Site or Profile	Key Information to Include	Things to Consider in Building Content
Professional profiles	• Work experience by company and position • Professional accomplishments • Skills and competencies • Personal traits and characteristics • Ways in which you have made a difference for clients or employer • Degrees, certifications • Awards, citations • Recommendations from colleagues, clients, managers • Publications, patents • Links to other sites	• Use the "story" format (by using "I" rather than your name) or neutral voice, as in a resume. • Display a photo depicting how you want employers or clients to perceive you. • As much as possible, show consistency in capability and expertise rather than touting yourself as a jack-of-all-trades. • Avoid empty language. • Avoid controversial topics such as strong religious or political sentiments.
Social profiles	• Groups and affiliations of personal interest. • Hobbies, favorite books, movies, things to do, etc. • Friends, contacts • Chat, banter, wall posts, ongoing discussions • Photos, video images, other forms of media	• Avoid unflattering or unprofessional photos, comments, and information. • Share news and information consistent with how you want to be perceived in personal and professional life. • Avoid posting about/discussing controversial topics

(continued)

Table 29.1   Continued

Type of Site or Profile	Key Information to Include	Things to Consider in Building Content
General search results	• Professional-related links, such as mentions in industry or general interest publications • White papers or other examples of thought leadership • Community or volunteer activities	• Set up a Google alert to monitor your online footprint. • Track and manage your online reputation regularly.

impression by any new association who does a search of your name online.

For the most part, strangers will take you the way you present yourself when you first meet. Your ability to establish rapport, earn their respect, engage them in meaningful conversation, and create a basis for further contact will carry the initial encounter. But as the Internet plays a greater role in vetting us—and information about individuals becomes widely and easily accessible—it's essential to establish a favorable online presence that reinforces and supports your in-person impression.

Chapter at a Glance

- Your new connection is likely to research you online after your initial encounter.
- Who you are online is a big part of who you are.
- Your web visibility and personality will either reinforce or diminish others' perceptions of you.
- Build an online presence that is consistent with how you present yourself in person, and that supports and reinforces the way you want others to think of you.

SECTION

IV

Gender-Neutral Random Connecting

As a male, I cannot claim to have walked the path—or for that matter, in the shoes—of a female random networker. However, I don't have to be a social scientist to know that there are unique considerations when random connecting across genders. I'm all in favor of using one's resources and tools to one's advantage—in other words, going with the best of what you've got—so the matter of random connecting between the sexes warrants special attention.

It's no secret that men and women see and think about the world differently. It's built, and then programmed, into us. Not to mention, there is the vibrational energy of male versus female; there's flirting energy, and there's professional business energy. And if you're a successful businesswoman or businessman, you surely know the difference, on both the giving and receiving ends. So although making random connections with complete strangers in any situation requires excellent interpersonal skills, those abilities are especially important when it comes to connecting across genders. I randomly connect with both men and women every day, because it is second nature for me to talk to strangers all the time— whether I'm in an elevator, at the grocery store checkout, waiting on a taxi line, or at any of the dozens of other day-to-day venues in which I find myself.

The electric frisson of meeting new people is the engine that drives my business. But I cannot claim expert status when it comes to making random business connections across the sexes. Sure, I have turned random encounters with women into profitable relationships, but since I can present only one side of the equation (that being decidedly male) with complete personal accuracy, I asked colleague, licensed social worker, and author Anne Driscoll to weigh in. Because Anne's work has examined gender relations— and because she has a distinctly female perspective—her input on this subject is incredibly valuable.

Below is a question-and-answer interview with Anne on the subject of cross-gender random connecting.

Q. Why does it matter that women and men pay attention to their differences when attempting to make random connections?

A. We spend our days weaving in and out of social situations— meeting, greeting, and interacting—men with women, women with women, women with men, and men with men. So gender is an ever-present factor. But we often take little or no conscious notice of what gender it is with whom we're relating. The truth is that, for the most part, it may matter very little whether or not the person who gets your coffee at Starbucks is a man or woman. However, it might matter a great deal when you're sipping that coffee in a first-class seat next to a prospective new client—and for some very good reasons.

Although the gender factor is so closely integrated into every-day experience that we almost don't pay it any mind, the fact is that men and women tend to see the world differently—and as such, potentially have distinct communication styles. Men and women are hardwired in dissimilar ways, a factor that deeply influences our interactions with and impressions of the world. And it can obviously have profound implications for our professional lives. Although it would be inaccurate to suggest that *all* men share certain traits and *all* women exhibit others, there is a growing body of research that demonstrates brain-based differences between boys and girls and between men and women.

Therefore, neglecting to pay attention to the differences between men's and women's communication styles can have some pretty dire consequences for random connecting. It can almost be as though two people who speak different languages are trying to communicate; not only won't they be able to convey their thoughts, they might even offend each other if they aren't careful. For example, women are generally (and I emphasize "generally," because there are surely exceptions) more attuned to beauty and aesthetics whereas men are typically more oriented toward the practical side of things. If you're a woman who wants to strike up a conversation with a man in an attempt to make a random business connection, you wouldn't want to start by pointing out how beautiful something is; you would probably be better off commenting on its usefulness or practicality. In other words, women tend to look at the garden, men are more likely to look first at the garage.

Many of these ideas are controversial, and it's understandable why. Since the birth of feminism, women have worked hard to prove that they are men's equal, deserving of every opportunity that men routinely get. So in the name of equality in the workplace—and in all fairness—there are no differences between the capability of men and women. So although men and women deserve equal opportunities, it's highly advisable for the random connector to recognize the differences in their *communication* styles and approaches to the world.

Q. So what are some of those differences men and women need to keep in mind when random connecting?

A. Women and men have varying filters in how they see the world. These are many and significant. For example, according to author and well-respected gender expert Michael Gurian, males are more likely to use deductive reasoning, whereas females tend toward inductive thinking. Therefore, if you are a woman and happen to share a cab with a prospective male client, you might pitch your capabilities with deductive rationale. And if you're a male talking to a female about her line of work, you might ask about her favorite parts of the job, rather than how she climbed the corporate ladder at her company.

By and large, research shows that women are better listeners, feel more comfortable in discussions, and are more intuitive than men. Studies have also found that females write, read, and speak more words than males, on average. So although it would be okay to take a longer route to your point if you are following up a random encounter with a woman through an e-mail, you should probably get directly to the point if you're communicating with a male.

Perhaps the most striking difference in communication styles between men and women is that women pay more attention to the emotional context of a conversation, whereas men tend to focus on facts and figures. Interestingly, we develop this emphasis over a lifetime, beginning at birth. In fact, one University of Cambridge study found that if 12-month-old boys are given the choice between watching people talking or windshield wipers moving, they tend to prefer the flapping wipers! Research went on to show that newborn girls are far better able to maintain eye contact than boys—another important difference to keep in mind later in life as we interact across genders as adults.

This generally points to a tendency for women to be more adept at reading and responding to social situations. That means men need to pay special attention to their interpersonal communication skills when interacting with a woman, whereas they may not need to work as hard at it when talking with another man.

Renowned psychologist Daniel Goleman has spent his career investigating emotional intelligence and says that overall women have the edge when it comes to self-awareness, management of emotions, empathy, and social skills.

However, men can be proficient in this area as well—and interestingly, the *men* who have these social skills and emotional intelligence tend to be the highest achievers.

Much of this area of research is unfolding, and many members of this field are still debating and defining the extent to which certain tendencies are innate or learned. In either case, there are differences, and wise is the random connector who gives them careful consideration.

So why is it important? Although it may not be necessary to become an expert on brain-based gender differences in order to land a profitable new association, you are likely to make more—and better—random connections if you become more aware of how men and women operate.

Q. What are some of those differences men and women need to keep in mind when random connecting?

A. Women and men have different filters through how they see and engage in the world—differences that are many and significant. For example, according to Michael Gurian, male brains are more likely to follow a logical line of thinking that suggests "if A, then B." Females, on the other hand, tend toward intuitive thinking; they reach a conclusion based on observing generalities.

It's my theory that women tend toward intuition because they're very much focused on relationships—between both people and things. An engineer friend told me recently that he was networking at a conference and found himself the sole man talking to an elite group of women executives. "It was fascinating, like being part of an inner society—they talked about their clothing, kids, and closets," he recalled. He picked up on those cues and became aware that in order to be in rapport with them, he had to tailor his conversation to theirs. He steered away from sports talk and instead discussed topics he knew would interest them, based on his experiences with his wife and daughters. For the same reason, he said that he would frame his conversation differently if he were to make a presentation in a random encounter for the encryption software his company sells depending on whether he was talking to a man or a woman. He'd plead a straightforward case with a man; perhaps by trying to persuade him that since his company is the leading provider of encryption programming to the government, the prospect's company would get more government certifications by using his company's software.

On the other hand, if he were randomly connecting with and trying to sell the same product to a woman, he'd probably emphasize relationship building. He'd likely suggest to her that the strategic relationships she has with vendors is essential and that since both his company and hers make complementary products, a small project would be a great way to pilot the relationship, and then just go from there.

Q. As a woman, what would you recommend that men do—or not do—when attempting to connect with you?

A. If you are approaching me, keep in mind that I am not your girlfriend, mother, sister, or wife. I am also not a prospective date, so lines you might practice in a bar are not likely to work with me—and even worse, may completely turn me off. Therefore, your tone of voice, your body language, and your conversation should convey the intention of what and why you're initiating the contact—and that is to make a *professional* connection.

Although many men may not realize this, even the strongest, most capable, most confident women can sometimes feel an undercurrent of vulnerability. Women are programmed from birth to be cautious and to protect themselves. This is something men don't think about as much, and have to constantly keep in mind when interacting with a woman, especially in random encounter situations. Women have to remain alert to risk and danger; it's something with which women must live daily. They know, for example, the inherent riskiness of walking alone on a street at night or being alone in a parking garage—things to which men might not give a second thought. Men need to be mindful of this outlook and make their communication clear, safe, and comfortable at all times.

However, nature has compensated for any limits women have in terms of physical prowess with—you got it—heightened emotional intelligence. And men would be well advised to keep in mind that women are generally adept at reading social situations and understanding a conversation's emotional context. Therefore, whenever a male approaches a woman he doesn't know, no matter what the circumstances, he should keep his tone neutral and nonthreatening and his demeanor professional and respectful. It's fine to be chatty and informal, but steer clear of anything too personal or intrusive. For example, let's say you're a man who is random connecting with a woman in a travel venue. Although it might be completely harmless to ask another man where he's staying, asking a woman that same question could raise red flags and hamper the conversation.

One of the ways that men can increase their chances of creating a nonthreatening interaction is by mirroring—simply reflecting back the tone, affect, and body language of the woman. For example, if a woman is sitting at a table, try to get at her eye level; this will probably create more comfort and rapport and therefore lead to a more successful conversation. And keep in mind that the same is true for women approaching men: mirroring is the grease of social interaction.

Q. What should women do—and not do—when they're trying to random connect with man?

A. Just as a man needs to keep his conversation on point when connecting with a woman, so too does a woman when approaching a man. If the goal is to uncover and advance business opportunities, women need to initiate conversation with men in a friendly, but not flirty, way. Women should avoid anything that smacks of sexual innuendo and keep the talk comfortable but professional. Be aware of body language that might be misinterpreted as flirtatious, such as playing with your hair, licking your lips, or touching a man's arm.

Just as men need to be mindful of how women experience the world, women should also be mindful of how men perceive the world and their communication styles. A touch on the arm could be easily misinterpreted by a man, leading in a direction the woman does not want to go.

In terms of content, men tend to be problem solvers, so a conversation that provides resolutions to problems works well. Focusing on a business issue or challenge you think he might have and posing a potential solution is very likely to get a male's attention. However, emotional appeals aren't going to be as effective. In most men's minds, logic is going to win out over feelings.

There are other dos and don'ts. Do smile, sound confident, and make eye contact (but not too much). If you want to be treated as an equal, act like one. It's not enough just to know your stuff. You have to show your stuff (and I don't mean cleavage!). I mean your competence. Men do this without thought—with bravado, even. Women, on the other hand, tend to be understated, something we've been taught and therefore something we think is appropriate. But you can't hide behind humility when you're attempting to professionally connect with someone. Showing that you mean business—and why—will increase your chances of turning an encounter into a profitable business opportunity.

Q. What are the biggest mistakes women make in attempting to random connect with men?

A. Women in the professional world are in a challenging position. We know from research, for example, that the more attractive you make yourself, the more likely you'll achieve success (something that's true for both men and women, by the way). So, on the one hand, women may try to optimize their attractiveness, yet at the same time, they have to not invite too much attention for their looks.

But I think women *should* play up their physical assets. By that I mean they should dress in a flattering way, wear stylish haircuts, and use makeup that enhances. Men and women are drawn to visual cues; therefore, it's all the better for both sexes to be visually attractive. But while being attractive is an asset, it alone is clearly not enough. You also need substance.

Mostly this requires that women keep in mind how men see the world. Remember, they like the bottom line, and they prefer to be direct. So don't allow the conversation to meander. Keep the interaction focused and on point. Chitchat is fine to a degree, but talking with a man and keeping him focused on the topic at hand requires different communication techniques than when talking with another woman.

Q. How should a woman respond when she's trying to make a random connection with a man who keeps trying to make it more personal than the woman wants?

A. Almost every woman has found herself in this position at one time or another. Fortunately, their social radar is so finely attuned to this that they usually pick up cues from a mile away, and before things go too far. In some ways, dealing with this type of situation requires the same skills necessary in dealing with children who want something they can't have. In short, you must redirect the conversation.

If a man asks personal questions that make a woman uncomfortable, the woman should gently guide the conversation back to where it belongs. Or do like politicians do and just ignore the question; answer instead with a topic that you want to address. Sometimes, a man will railroad over these maneuvers; in that case, a woman will have to be blunter and say, "I'd prefer to discuss how my product might help your business" or "My flight is about to board, so I'd really rather use the time we have left to talk about your company and how I might be able to help it." That overt, clear redirection of the conversation will set an unmistakable boundary and keep things on a professional level.

Q. Is there a place for flirting in making random encounters when the goal is purely business related?

A. No, at least not if you intend to have an interaction that leads to a business relationship. Does that mean conversations never take on a "flirty" tone? No, it doesn't. In fact, some people come across that way thinking it's to their advantage. But flirtatiousness is not appropriate for professionals of either gender who are seeking business connections. It is far more likely to work against the person. Sure, we should all use our natural attributes to our advantage— a good sense of humor, a witty mind, a great smile—to help advance the connection. But that doesn't include sex appeal. It all comes down to what you want from the connection.

If it's purely business, it should be kept that way. If there's an undeniable personal chemistry that spills over, it's up to both parties to decide what to do about it. But if you want to be respected for your professional abilities, and if you want to keep the new connection going toward a profitable business relationship, the key is to understand the difference between how men and women see and communicate about the world, and to use that insight to expand your professional opportunities.

SECTION

V

Mastery Insights and the *Talk to Strangers Mastery Program*

So far you have learned about what kind of attitudes and skills it takes to turn everyday travels into big opportunities to expand your business, career, income, and life. Yet as with every skill, there is a level of mastery at which one is able to demonstrate the skills with great proficiency, leading to more success than when one is just beginning. Webster's dictionary defines *mastery* as "possession or display of great skill." When it comes to random connecting, *mastery* translates into random encounters that generate greater results faster—and with more ease.

Of course, the definition of achieving a great result depends on what you're going for, but the difference between a master random connector and someone who has just average ability is that the master will get the name of a higher level influencer when seeking a contact from the new acquaintance. If attempting to sell a product, the master connector is likely to make a bigger deal. If seeking an investor, the amount of the investment will be larger, and if selling consulting services, the scope of the engagement will be broader.

In addition, a master random connector will achieve all of these results faster than an average one. The master will identify the opportunity more quickly, begin the conversation about it earlier, and seal the deal more often—and do it all with greater ease. There's more to random connecting mastery, so read on and challenge yourself to achieve excellence.

Mastery in any skill or topic typically occurs at an unconscious level; in other words, you're so good at something you don't even know how you got to be so good. You do it without trying or conscious awareness; it's simply become second nature. Some might think of mastery as a form of honed intuition that comes with a sense of mindlessness. Being able to do things at a high level of competency without having to try very hard is the level we all want to realize in terms of the skills that are important to us.

However, reaching that level of capability clearly doesn't happen overnight; it takes time and effort to achieve. There is an old story of the tourist walking in Manhattan who stops a man on the street and asks, "Excuse me, but do you know how to get to Carnegie Hall?" to which the man responds, "Practice, practice, practice!" The same is true for mastering your random connecting skills. By practicing—sometimes getting it right, sometimes getting it wrong and adjusting your technique accordingly—you will eventually reach the level where you are making new connections all the time, a higher percentage of which are with influential people. In addition, you are leveraging your new connections into life-changing outcomes more frequently and predictably.

This section will show you what random connecting mastery represents for you, why it's worth mastering, and how you can achieve that degree of proficiency so that you can draw upon and demonstrate it at any time.

Mastery Point 1: You Live—Really *Live*—the Four Beliefs of Successful Random Connectors

Opportunities don't come to those who wait; they come to those who *create* them. Your ability to expand your world through new people and possibilities comes through the mind-set you carry with you wherever you go. The foundation of all the other skills and behaviors of random connecting is in your ability to embrace these four tenets, integrate them into your unconscious mind, and act from them in your daily encounters. When you truly believe in your bones that the world is a friendly place—that you can meet anyone, that everyone you meet has value to you, and that you have value to everyone you meet—all the other skills will fall into place more easily.

Mastery Point 2: You Are Naturally and Fundamentally Flexible

Throughout your random connecting experiences, you will encounter a wide range of personalities and communication styles. Your ability to connect successfully with each of these types of individuals will require mental and behavioral agility. Master random connectors are not locked in to any single, particular style of interacting with others; rather, you are highly responsive to the other person and able to modify your personality and communication to match the other's. This core trait will allow you to succeed with any situation or person, regardless of how similar or different the other person is from you. And although mirroring is a vital way to create rapport and alignment, flexibility is the core trait that enables you to do it successfully in all circumstances, with all personality types.

Mastery Point 3: You Are Fearless

The very nature of random connecting is daunting for some people. The notion of reaching out to complete strangers in public places is about as comfortable as putting their hand in a shark tank. No doubt, meeting strangers takes courage. But once you are equipped with the knowledge and skills you've acquired through this book, you will approach the world with more confidence. And the master random connector fears no venue. "Let me at 'em," thinks the true pro. "I can meet anyone, anywhere." A master will confidently take on any circumstance. If someone piques your curiosity 10 rows back in the plane, you'll find a way to talk with him or her. If you overhear someone on the other side of a coffee shop saying something on a cell phone that catches your interest, you'll find a way to meet. If someone gets on the elevator wearing a logo from a company you want to do business with, you'll come up with something to say and ultimately get that person's contact info. That is the kind of fearlessness that comes with random connecting mastery.

Mastery Point 4: You Can Pick Out the Best Potential Connection in the Crowd

You'll often find yourself in a situation with many potential new contacts to whom you could talk; however, some will clearly be more valuable than others. You have a choice of who to approach and with whom you can start a conversation. Earlier in the book, we discussed the dangers of judging people from a distance based on external, superficial observation. Although conversation clues can surely guide you and help make the decision easier, the fact is that some people in the room (or on the plane or on the line or at the bar) represent greater opportunity for you than others do. Master random connectors are able to zone in on exactly who those people are. They have a sixth sense that lets them know to whom they should direct their attention and strike up the million-dollar conversation.

Mastery Point 5: You Create Comfort and Trust Quickly

When you approach complete strangers and begin talking, they will decide whether you are safe in that first split second of interaction. They will determine whether they can trust you, if they are comfortable with you, and if they should open up to you. When you become a master random connector, you will instinctively be able to get on others' wavelengths and create a sense of safety and comfort. You will bring a nonthreatening energy or chemistry that engenders trust. And you will do it literally within the very first seconds of your interaction.

Mastery Point 6: You Know Just the Right Thing to Say to Start the Conversation

The first words that come out of your mouth will set the stage for the interaction. As you learned earlier in the book, you can say something about the circumstance; you can give a conversation clue, discuss a shared common experience, or use any of a number of other opening lines. But the master is able to say that perfect thing that resonates deeply with the other person. The master makes a statement that captures his or her experience or truth in that moment, almost stopping others in their tracks and causing them to take note and respond. "Yes, that is exactly what I was thinking, too." They might even ask, "Yes, how did you know?" in response. Part of saying just the right thing is in *what* you say; the other part is in how you say it.

Mastery Point 7: You Describe Yourself and the Value You Offer in an Irresistible Way

At some point in the conversation you will have your chance to position yourself and your capabilities in a way that allows your new connection to perceive the value you can bring to him or her. A master random connector doesn't just say what he or she does but explains it in a way the other person finds undeniably compelling. You describe your product, service, knowledge, resources—or whatever comprises your offerings—so persuasively and congruently with the other person's needs that he or she immediately recognizes its value. You show that you can do something for that person that is unique, relevant, and so focused on how he or she will benefit as a result that that person absolutely *has* to have it.

Mastery Point 8: You Are Able to Identify the Leverage Point Quickly, While Being Respectful to the Other Person

You will be scanning for how your new acquaintance can be of value to you—and you to him or her—during your conversation. As you talk, ask, listen, and respond, you will discover if and how there is a basis for further interaction. However, as we discovered earlier in this book, no one wants to feel that they're being used solely for their power or influence. The master random connector is able to zero in on the leverage point quickly while preserving the integrity of the relationship. A master connector is able to determine whether there's anything there while ensuring that the other person feels respected and valued for who he or she is—not just for his or her connections or influence.

Mastery Point 9: Your Follow-up Leads to Action and Commitment From the Other Party (aka "Closes the Deal") Quickly . . . and Often

Interesting conversations among interesting people make life, well . . . interesting. And no doubt, people all over the world have fun, stimulating, and engaging exchanges with strangers every day. But the ultimate sign of random connecting mastery is in the ability to turn that new association into a mutually productive, profitable outcome more often than not. The master maintains contact, keeps the momentum of the initial meeting going, builds personal credibility, and cultivates the interpersonal relationship so that the connection manifests into something tangible almost every time. The master random connector pursues those random encounters that represent the greatest opportunity and knows how to realize them quickly and often.

All of these abilities came together for me recently when I turned a four-minute random encounter with a complete stranger in a hectic airport concourse into a profitable consulting engagement within four months of the initial meeting.

Time was not on my side, with people hurriedly heading for their flights, grabbing at the one chance for decent food before boarding. I struck up a conversation with a man who was getting ready to leave the food kiosk as I was arriving. We made eye contact and exchanged a nod of acknowledgment, which I followed up with a smile and the comment: "That's what I call eating on the run."

To this he replied, "Yeah, it's hardly gourmet, but it sure beats a bag of pretzels."

We chuckled in that common understanding. "Where are you headed?" I asked.

"Washington, DC," he said.

"Ah. Do you work for the government?" When he replied affirmatively, I said with enthusiasm, "Wow, that's great . . . which agency or department?"

He answered and went on to tell me about the kind of work he does and described an upcoming project he'll be working on. I drilled down with genuine curiosity and determined that there could be a good fit for my expertise. "That sounds like an exciting initiative," I said. "I specialize in that area and have a lot of experience with projects like that. I wonder if we could exchange cards and if I could follow up and talk some more about it. You never know where that could lead."

"Sure," he said, as he reached into his briefcase and pulled out a card. I did the same.

Within those four minutes and a handful of sentences, I established rapport, found out where he lived and worked as well as what type of work he did, discovered that he had a project for which I might be a good fit, obtained his contact info, gave him mine, and gained agreement to follow up and talk again.

Upon returning to my office, I sent him an e-mail restating parts of our conversation and suggesting some specific ways I could be of assistance with his project, to which he responded that he was interested. We then scheduled an appointment to talk on the phone, which we did. I followed that up with another e-mail that included a proposal. We spoke one more time, and within two months, I was spec'd into an extended consulting engagement. It is a perfect example of what is possible when we apply the principles and techniques of random connecting to our everyday lives.

The *Talk to Strangers Mastery Program*

Networking has found its way to the front and center of the professional world, since *who* you know is often more important than *what* you know. Savvy, successful people have come to realize that they can increase their pool of opportunities by expanding their universe of contacts. Yet it's often in the unpredictable, unplanned, random meetings in everyday interactions that we make the most powerful connections. The *Talk to Strangers Mastery Program*—a step-by-step plan for mastering the art and science of turning random encounters into productive, life-changing relationships— follows. This program will help you achieve the highest level of proficiency in turning those encounters into mutually profitable, productive relationships.

Step 1: Become Aware of the Potential in Your Everyday Encounters

Although traditional networking is good for making contacts within an industry or marketplace, you have an untapped world of potential in the people you meet in serendipitous, random inter-actions from the moment you walk out your door every day. The first step in tapping this huge pool of opportunity is to begin to recognize the opportunities that exist in the people you encounter every day.

Consider or answer . . .

- How often do you start conversations with people you don't know in everyday random venues?
- Have you had experiences where you met a stranger and ended up making a productive connection? Do you know of others who've had such an experience?
- What, if anything, might be keeping you from initiating con-versations with strangers in your everyday life?

Practice . . .

For the next week, pay special attention to how many people you encounter in your day-to-day life and begin striking up conversations with as many of them as you can.

Step 2: Bring Transparency to All of Your Interactions With Others

There is usually only a thin veneer separating strangers from potential friends or associates. People are available just below the surface more often than not, and they usually seek human connection with others. By sharing just a little bit of yourself and giving others permission to do the same, you create a pathway for unlimited opportunity through the people you encounter in your everyday life.

> *Consider or answer . . .*
> - Why do you think transparency is so important in meeting people, especially ones who can help you in your professional or personal life?
> - Who do you know who you think is particularly transparent?
> - How open are you to sharing your thoughts and feelings with people you don't know very well?
> - What would you need to do to become more transparent with people you have just met?

Practice . . .
For the next week, share just a little more information about yourself than you typically would; notice how it feels and how it influences how others respond to you.

Step 3: Live the Four Beliefs of Successful Random Connectors

When you truly believe that the world is a friendly place where people—even strangers—are available to you, that just about everyone you see in a public place can be met, that everyone you meet can enhance your life, and finally, that you can enhance theirs as well, you will have knowledge you can turn into action that expands your life in ways you could never even predict.

Consider or answer . . .

- What evidence is there of the fact that the world *is* a friendly place?
- Have you ever seen someone you didn't know in an every-day encounter whom you wanted to connect with but you thought the person wasn't available? Would you have attempted to meet the person if you had the knowledge and insight from this book?
- If you could make a new contact today who would be of the greatest value to you, who would that be and what would you ask that person for?
- What are three ways that you can enrich someone else's life?

Practice . . .
For each day during the four days, pick one of the four beliefs and pay special attention to living it that day.

Step 4: Go Beyond Your Comfort Zone; Seek New Faces in New Places

We all tend to follow the same routes and spend our time in the same locations where we are most familiar. We are creatures of habit, frequenting those venues where we feel safe and comfort-able. Yet if you want to find new and untapped power portals, you will want to continually put yourself in new venues where you are likely to find new people—and therefore, new opportunities.

Consider or answer . . .

- What are the five most common places you go in your day-to-day life where you are around other people? Include their exact locations. Consider a different location for each one where you could go or explore.

Practice . . .

Do three of the following during the next week:

- Stop at a different coffee shop.
- Shop at a different supermarket.
- Sit in a different section of the train or bus.
- Sit in a different section of your favorite restaurant or bar.
- Take a different route to work.
- Stand in a different area of the sporting event with your children.
- Expand your social network and make new friends by reaching out to work colleagues, neighbors, and/or friends of friends and make a social appointment.

Step 5: Watch for Access Clues in the People You See Around You

Transcending the veil from stranger to potential connection requires thought and skill. Although the vast majority of people are available just under the surface, they are more likely to respond favorably when you approach them respectfully and gently. The good news is that people give off clues about themselves; some are obvious, whereas others are more subtle. Some of these signals of accessibility include company logos on shirts, laminated business cards on briefcases, and embroidered conference or convention names and dates on backpacks. All of these give you content you can use for breaking the ice.

Consider or answer . . .

- What are some ways people reveal information about themselves that you can use to start a conversation?

Practice . . .

For this week, see how much you can discover about the people you see around you or encounter in your day-to-day life, simply by noticing what information they make available about themselves without even speaking.

Step 6: Break the Ice and Make a Connection

Although it is easier to pierce the veil of isolation than you think, people decide in the first few seconds whether they think you're someone they want to converse with or not. Do you make them feel comfortable? Can they trust you? Do they like you? These are instant and instinctive questions they will ask themselves. The first thing you say—and the way in which you say it—will determine whether there is an opportunity for further conversation. An observation about what is happening in the moment around you both, a question that demonstrates authentic curiosity on your part, or a comment that will resonate with what the other person is doing are all opening lines that, when said in a comforting, safe way, will create the space you need to have an engaging and meaningful exchange—one that allows you to discover all that is possible through your newfound connection.

Consider or answer . . .
- What do you consider to be the difference between something that a new acquaintance can say that would engender comfort and interest and something that would prevent you from engaging in conversation?
- What are some safe and intriguing statements you can make to spark someone's interest and enhance his or her desire to continue a conversation with you?

Practice . . .
For the next three days, strike up a conversation with at least one new person you come across in a random, daily encounter. For the four following days, make at least two new connections with complete strangers.

Step 7: Guide the Conversation Toward the *Most Productive Outcome*

Everyone you meet has something to offer. Sometimes it's through their direct influence—to buy something, to hire you, to invest in your business, and so on. Other times, it is via their professional connections; perhaps you want them to introduce you to someone of influence or authority. And sometimes it's through their family members or personal contacts. To discover how an individual can be of greatest value to you—the power portal—you will want to demonstrate authentic curiosity and respectfully direct the conversation so that you can gather the information you need to assess this person's degree and/or type of influence.

Consider or answer . . .
- What would you want to find out about someone you meet in an everyday encounter that would let you know if, and how, that person could be of value to you?
- What questions could you ask that would gently uncover this key information?
- How can you tell when someone is being authentically curious versus feigning interest?

Practice . . .
Over the next three days, practice being curious about people you don't know by asking them questions about themselves, covering topics such as their line of work, their company, where they like to vacation, where they went to college, where they were raised, and/or what they thought of the last book they read or movie they saw. For the following four days, meet at least two new people and discover a way they can be of value to you, either through their own influence or through someone they know of influence.

Step 8: Present Yourself as a Value Proposition

Just as the people you meet have value to you, you also have value
to them. That is a central tenet of turning everyday encounters
into mutually profitable relationships. People won't buy from you,
hire you, introduce you to others who have influence, or otherwise
invest their time or money in you unless—and until—you show
them that you have something of value to offer in return. This is
your value proposition, and it comes through your product or service, your knowledge, your skills, your experience, your ability to
make money for others, or any number of other ways you create
value for others.

Consider or answer . . .
- What do you do, know, or provide that makes a positive difference to others?
- Make a list of the *specific* ways your product, service, expertise,
  or offering translates into value for others.

Practice . . .
Notice how many times this week, and in what ways, you and
  your activities—either professionally or personally—positively
  affected others, be they colleagues, customers, neighbors,
  friends, or anyone else you interact with professionally or
  personally.

Step 9: Follow Up/Leverage the Connection

Meeting new people and discovering the power portals in your
everyday life gets you only halfway to your goal. You have to capi-
talize on the connection to make it across the finish line. Until
you leverage your new contact, you have made only a friend. And
although friends are treasures in their own right—and sometimes
the most valuable relationships begin as friendships—successful

opportunity expansionists are focused on determining how to monetize the relationship. Once you have identified how this person can be of value to you and you to him or her, you will want to follow up with an e-mail, phone call, or note where you direct the next step toward whatever opportunity was unearthed in your initial encounter. Sometimes a proposal is appropriate; sometimes it's simply another step in the process. But always it should move the relationship—and the opportunity—forward.

Consider or answer . . .
- How do you think a follow-up note nurtures a relationship?
- What "next step" could you propose after meeting your ideal new connection?
- What mode of communication, e-mail, voice mail, snail mail, phone, or in-person, do you think has the greatest impact for a follow-up?

Practice . . .
For the next week, make a point of following up on one new encounter each day. Reference the meeting, recap the conversation, and propose a next step that will bring you closer to monetizing the connection.

Step 10: Make Everyday Encounters a Way of Life for the Rest of Your Life

It will always be through the people we meet and get to know that we are able to monetize opportunities and realize our hopes and dreams. The awareness and techniques you have developed here should provide you with a capability that will serve you for as long as you want to expand your business, career, income, and life. The minute you leave your house each day, you step into a world full of power portals—and you will find them wherever you go if you keep your eyes, ears, and mind open.

Consider or answer...

- Which parts of all the skills you have learned in this book have been the most difficult to embrace or implement? Which have been the easiest?
- What, if anything, would keep you from embracing or implementing the principles and methods presented in this program?
- How many new connections do you think it is reasonable to discover through everyday encounters on a weekly or monthly basis?

Practice...

For this week—and as a standard practice in your life—apply the skills and techniques of this program and strive for mastery. This will allow you to achieve unlimited success in expanding your business, your career, your income, and your life.

Conclusion

"The world is my oyster" is an often-quoted line from Shakespeare's *The Merry Wives of Windsor,* and it has been adapted to modern times to remind us that opportunity is all around us, if only we will make the effort to open up to it.

If you want to expand your life by expanding your universe of connections, you need look no further than the person sitting or standing next to you, behind you, or across the room from you, every single day. All it takes is the courage to take the road less traveled, to invite conversation, to tap into the desire we all have for direct human contact—even as we text on our smartphones and tap away on our computer keyboards.

I leave home every day believing the world is a friendly place, that I can meet just about anyone, that everyone I come across has something to offer, and that I, too, have value to give. And whether the opportunity is obvious or not, the potential is for money or friendship, immediate or long term, I have enriched my business, my career, my income, and my life through those I've encountered, right outside my door.

It always has been, and always will be, through the people we meet and know that we achieve our goals and expand our lives. We can't do it alone. So when we meet someone who can help us along in our journeys, if we can return some value in kind, it is more than likely a perfect chance to find the pearl that sits waiting inside the oyster that is your world.

Index